OPEN HEAVEN

The Transformation

Clive Pick

ISBN 0-9737133-0-5

2nd printing in Canada by Crossroads Christian Communications Inc. // Visualeyes Communications

Dedication

It is with great joy and love that I dedicate this book to my dear Mother, who has been such a blessing and support to both myself, and my wife Esther, and also to the call on our lives. When I was fourteen years old my Mother explained to me that as a born-again Christian I should start to tithe, which I have obediently done ever since. This has released such tremendous blessing into my life, and I now have the privilege of teaching others what my Mother trained me in.

> *"Train up a child in the way he should go, and when he is old he will not depart from it."*
>
> (Proverbs 22:6)

To my wife Esther, this book would not have been possible without your love, your commitment, and your dedication to both The Lord and to me. Thank you.

Foreword

My brief lunch meeting with Clive Pick turned into a powerful, three-hour session that culminated in a meaningful time of prayer in my office. As Clive was sharing with me the economic principles of God's Kingdom, his words resonated in my spirit. I sensed the Lord clearly speaking to me that this was a pivotal message for His Church...a message of vital importance in preparing God's people to receive the greatest harvest of souls we have ever seen. That day had a profound impact on my life and ministry.

Since that time with Clive, he has tremendously blessed our staff at Crossroads through a series of teaching seminars similar to those he has been sharing around the world during his many years of ministry. I have also spent time with Clive at his home and on 100 Huntley Street, delving into this concept of "The Open Heaven." In a day where much teaching about money seems to be motivated by a self-centred seeking of prosperity, Clive brings a balanced, Biblical breath of fresh air. I have found him to be a humble man who speaks gently but with much spiritual authority and with a clear anointing by God for this hour.

Clive and his dear wife Esther felt compelled by God to move to Canada recently, because they know God is on the brink of something BIG in this country...something we all need to plug into. The bottom line factor is our obedience. As you read Open Heaven: The Transformation, do so with an open heart, and as you are challenged in your spirit to take a step of faith, go for it! It's time for every follower of Jesus to experience the abundance and multiplication that God longs to pour down from the "windows of heaven" into our lives and through us out to others.

Rev. Ron Mainse
President, Crossroads Christian Communications Inc.
Host of 100 Huntley Street

Introduction

We are seeing the body of Christ being renewed by the power of the Holy Spirit, but there is also another work being done by Him: a work that is so vital in these last days. Father is releasing finance to His people, for the preparation and the return of His Son. As we are obedient and understand the word of God regarding His financial system, the body of Christ will see a total change in their financial situation.

You may be struggling financially at the moment, you may be in debt, or you may well be flowing in financial freedom. Whatever your situation you are about to see an increase, if you will only submit your finances to God.

Father has commissioned me to write this book, and it has been a three-year battle to put "word to paper." My wife Esther was continually sick for a year. She has also had to fight a stubborn computer as well as many other distractions, as she faithfully copied and edited my written manuscript.

I know that as you read this book, you will discover the keys to your own financial breakthrough. We are in a divine time-slot for the miraculous to happen. Please embrace what Father is saying to you.

Contents

Prologue

The Transformation

The season we are in is the season for The Father to release blessing to His people. When I speak of blessings, please do not just focus on dollars ! Blessings are the total favor of God on your life. God's covenant with you and I is to bless us, so that we can then be a blessing to others. God never created you to struggle, or to be in debt, or to be affected by poverty. The first thing that God did when He created man, was to bless him.

> *"So God created man in His own image; in the image of God He created him; male and female He created them. Then God blessed them, and God said to them, 'Be fruitful and multiply; fill the earth and subdue it; have dominion over the fish of the sea, over the birds of the air, and over every living thing that moves on the earth.'"*
>
> (Gen 1:27-28)

I have numerous documented testimonies on file from around the world. The following are just a few of the testimony quotes from brothers and sisters who have understood and been obedient to God's word on finance.

- Debts cancelled over-night.
- Monies being received from unexpected sources.
- In obedience to the teaching, churches have experienced a higher anointing for evangelism, and for healing.
- All manner of blessings that have been held back are suddenly released.
- Overall financial breakthrough.
- Total release from the "fear of giving."
- Sunday offerings increasing by 100% and "rising steadily."
- Money released to sow back into the gospel.
- A medical diagnosis of "anxiety" gone after clear teaching about finance which in return released the financial situation considerably
- Great rises of faith and expectancy.
- Houses, cars, and jobs released. One job release came after six years of unemployment, and another came after ten years.
- Dramatic increases in Christian businesses. "My business volume has doubled."
- Immigration papers released.
- From a new understanding of God's provision - visions have been released.
- After sowing in faith for a specific purpose monies have been released.
- Physical healing has manifested - as a result of an open heaven.
- The intimate side of marriages healed.
- Some church mortgages were paid up "years before the due date." Some church mortgages were cleared completely.
- Some churches reported that their income has tripled.
- The spiritual bondages of debt and poverty broken.
- Bible college students have had their fees paid.

Chapter 1

Abraham's Blessings are Yours

The law of inheritance is greater than the law of possession!
Abraham's blessings are ours by reason of a covenant promise
from God to Abraham.

> *"What I mean is this: The law, introduced 430 years
> later, does not set aside the covenant previously
> established by God and thus do away with the promise.
> For if the inheritance depends on the law, then it no
> longer depends on a promise; but God in his grace gave
> it to Abraham through a promise. ... Now that faith has
> come, we are no longer under the supervision of the
> law."*
>
> (Galatians 3:17-18, 25 NIV)

> *"I will bless those who bless you, and I will curse him
> who curses you; and in you all the families of the earth
> shall be blessed."*
>
> (Genesis 12:3)

> *"Now to Abraham and his Seed were the promises made.
> He does not say, 'And to seeds,' as of many, but as of
> one, 'And to your Seed,' who is Christ."*
>
> (Galatians 3:16)

This promise was not to all descendants of Abraham. It found
its fulfillment in Christ and in those who are united with Him.

"And if you are Christ's, then you are Abraham's seed, and heirs according to the promise."

(Galatians 3:29)

As a child of God this is your inheritance. This promise has given us an inheritance of continued blessings, but they come by our own free choice,

"I call heaven and earth as witnesses today against you, that I have set before you life and death, blessing and cursing; therefore choose life, that both you and your descendants may live."

(Deuteronomy 30:19)

These blessings can be blessings of finance, health, marriage, success in whatever you put your hands to; in fact every area of your life will be blessed, when you are obedient to God's principles. God will act on His covenant promise which is binding. The word tells us that now we have a better promise:

"But now He has obtained a more excellent ministry, in as much as He is also Mediator of a better covenant, which was established on better promises."

(Hebrews 8:6)

Under the new covenant, the promises have been increased, and they are yours to be claimed. The definition of "claim" is "to demand as rightfully belonging to you – a right to something." Child of God, please do not let the devil deceive you, or steal from you any longer. Now you know and understand that Abraham's blessings are yours. As you read on I believe that you will be released into all the blessings that Father God has for you.

The key word is "understand," for the measure in which you understand is the measure in which you will receive.

"Get wisdom! Get understanding! Do not forget, nor turn away from the words of my mouth."

(Proverbs 4:5)

Re-Establishing the Covenant of Blessings

Bringing a change to your financial situation can only come about by you doing it God's way! Not by you deciding to modify or adapt what God has laid down in His word. Remember the devil is a legalist. If you **do not give him any authority** at all with your finances, **he can take no authority**. Abraham is our pattern, and if we follow exactly what God told Abraham to do, we will then by inheritance, receive Abraham's blessings. The pattern was in this order, firstly to tithe, secondly to walk blameless before God, and finally to give an offering. I know that if we, the children of God follow this pattern, we will indeed receive our rightful inheritance.

"And if you are Christ's then you are Abraham's seed, and heirs according to the promise."

(Galatians 3:29)

To re-establish or to activate this covenant you need to understand, and be totally obedient to the three parts of the covenant.

The three parts are:

1. the tithe,
2. walking blameless before God, and
3. our offerings.

Part 1 - The Tithe

"Then Melchizedek king of Salem brought out bread and wine; he was the priest of God Most High. And he blessed him and said: "Blessed be Abram of God Most High, Possessor of heaven and earth; And blessed be God Most High, who has delivered your enemies into your hand." And he gave him a tithe of all."

(Genesis 14:18-20)

Start to tithe on every part of your income. On your gross salary before tax. Any family income support, child benefit, family credit, or job-seekers allowance. Any governmental assistance, any inheritances or bonuses, any tax returns, or monetary gifts, such as Christmas or birthday money, in fact **any financial increase** which comes into your life. The tithe is **not** an offering, it is God's money and must be returned to Him in full. This must be done weekly or monthly, including December! If we are not able to return to God His tithe of 10%, how then can we really expect God to return to us the wealth of the sinner?

Part 2 - Walking Blameless

> *"When Abram was ninety-nine years old, the LORD appeared to Abram and said to him, 'I am Almighty God; walk before Me and be blameless. And I will make My covenant between Me and you, and will multiply you exceedingly.'"*

(Genesis 17:1-2)

The important key here I believe is that before God asked Abram for an offering, He asked him to walk before Him blameless – I am purely focusing on financial blamelessness, because that is the area we are discussing and it is also the area that you are wanting your breakthrough in.

This blamelessness can be achieved for example, by not offering to do, or offering to pay cash for jobs done for us, or by us, to possibly avoid payment of any government taxation. All government taxation must be paid. Jesus said:

> *"Render therefore to Caesar the things that are Caesar's, and to God the things that are God's."*

(Matthew 22:21)

12

Please remember that some things that we did when we were in the world and were seen as socially acceptable are now not. There are many examples, and I know that God will speak to your hearts, if there are still areas known or unknown that need addressing. Here are just a couple of examples to show you how easy it can be to give Satan ground.

1.   When we leave a car park, and offer to give someone our ticket still showing time available when the ticket clearly states that it is non-transferable. It means that we cannot accept time on a ticket from anyone either, as we would have deprived the car park company of revenue.

2.   Accepting too much change from a cashier at a store, or even realizing that we have not been charged for one or more items. This is not a blessing from God, it means that the store would be out of pocket for the items not accounted for. Satan is a legalist and any form of robbery however small will block your blessings from God. I firmly believe that a **small discrepancy** can stop a **big blessing**...

> *"Catch us the foxes, the little foxes that spoil the vines, for our vines have tender grapes."*
>
> (Song of Songs 2:15)

Part 3 - The Offering

> *"Now it came to pass after these things that God tested Abraham, and said to him, 'Abraham!' And he said, 'Here I am.' Then He said, "Take now your son, your only son Isaac, whom you love, and go to the land of Moriah, and offer him there as a burnt offering on one of the mountains of which I shall tell you."*
>
> (Genesis 22:1-2)

God asked for a special offering from a 'blameless' Abraham. Remember the word "offering" means "to present for acceptance or consideration." We must therefore assume that God can if He so wishes refuse our offering, as He did to Cain. Remember man will always accept your offering, but God may not! Brothers and sisters, honestly ask yourself if God really can accept an offering from us that has been gained illegally.

> *"You shall not sow your vineyard with different kinds of seed, lest the yield of the seed which you have sown and the fruit of your vineyard be defiled."*
>
> (Deuteronomy 22:9)

Your financial breakthrough will come as you apply the following. Firstly repent of not tithing, and start to tithe in to the church where you worship. Secondly repent of financial unrighteousness and purpose in your heart to be accurate in your handling of money. Thirdly do pray about the amount of offering that you should give. When these three principles are followed your offerings will be acceptable to the Lord, and will then in turn activate your increase. To summarize the covenant of blessings:

- **the tithe will protect you financially,**
- **your integrity will position you financially, and**
- **your offerings will increase you financially.**

Your breakthrough is guaranteed according to the word of God. Remember it is not so much what we have to do to release God's blessings, but more a question of what is preventing God's blessings from reaching us.

Let us look at exactly what a covenant is. It is an agreement between two people or two groups that involves promises on the part of one to the other. The purpose of a covenant between God and His people is one of the most important truths in the Bible. By making a covenant with Abraham, God has promised to bless His descendants and to make them His special people. Abraham's part of the covenant, like ours, was to remain faithful and obedient to God and His word, and to serve as a channel through which God's blessings could flow to the rest of the world:

"In your seed all the nations of the earth shall be blessed, because you have obeyed My voice."

(Genesis 22:18)

The devil cannot stop our blessings. The only person that can stop our blessings is us! We can stop them by being disobedient to the word of God, or disobedient to something that Father God has asked us to do.

I would like at this point to ask you two questions and would then like you to answer them audibly.

1. Do you believe that Jesus is coming back soon for His church?
2. Do you believe that Jesus is coming back in your life time?

Many of you have answered yes to both questions. I believe if you have answered yes, that positive reply has come firmly out of your spirit, by revelation from the Holy Spirit. The Holy Spirit is preparing the body of Christ for the return of the bridegroom, and then for the glorious rapture of Jesus' church. If then we truly do believe that He will be back soon, we surely must commit ourselves, and our finances to God. We begin by changing our hearts, and our attitudes, and then by coming to know and understand, that we are the ones that must finance the end-time harvest.

Chapter 2

The Cash-less Society

The body of Christ has been waiting for nearly two thousand years for Jesus to return. I truly believe that we are the generation that will indeed see His return. As we look at signs around the world, we see clear evidence of biblical prophesy being fulfilled. There is a new excitement and expectation amongst God's people. The bride of Christ is preparing herself. The disciples themselves asked Jesus when He would return. Jesus told them:

> *"But of that day and hour no one knows, not even the angels of heaven, but My Father only. But as the days of Noah were, so also will the coming of the Son of Man be."*
> (Matthew 24:36-37)

This scripture tells us that when the Lord does return it will be sudden. But for those who look at the signs of the times, for those who read and understand the word of God, there will be a time for preparation. As we see from this scripture, it will be just as it was in Noah's days.

> *"Then the LORD saw that the wickedness of man was great in the earth, and that every intent of the thoughts of his heart was only evil continually."*
> (Genesis 6:5)

The happenings of those days are clearly in evidence today. The world would appear to be sex-crazed, and there is little if any regard for morality just "as in the days of Noah." The method the Lord used to purge the world was to flood it. Just think – that which He created He had to destroy. This was a phenomenon, something that had never happened before. The people had at that time no comprehension of a "flood" because there had never been rain on the earth. God opened the windows of heaven.

> *"In the six hundredth year of Noah's life, in the second month, the seventeenth day of the month, on that day all the fountains of the great deep were broken up, and the windows of heaven were opened. And the rain was on the earth forty days and forty nights."*
>
> (Genesis 7:11-12)

My personal belief is that just as the flood happened in those days, and affected the whole world, the Lord is telling us that there will be another phenomenon. Something that the world has never seen before. I believe that this unique happening that the world will witness will be the "cash-less society."

The first stages are already in motion in various places across the world. Very soon we will see the total withdrawal of cash. We the church of Jesus Christ are preparing for His return, and we all know it. The world are preparing for the rise of the anti-christ and they do not know it.

> *"And he said, "Go your way, Daniel, for the words are closed up and sealed till the time of the end. Many shall be purified, made white, and refined, but the wicked shall do wickedly; and none of the wicked shall understand, but the wise shall understand."*
>
> (Daniel 12:9-10)

Sadly the world have no idea of what is happening around them, nor of what is to come, which is why it is imperative for us to spread the good news, and to share the clear undiluted gospel of Jesus Christ to an otherwise lost world.

Each country throughout the world has its own financial structure. They have their own personal system of economics that works for them, and pays for the running of the country. Each country has various taxes for various things, not necessarily the same as other countries. Sad to say though, most countries throughout the world are teetering on the brink of financial disaster. Brothers and sisters, we do not come from a "country" we come from a **kingdom**, the Kingdom of God. God's Kingdom also has its own economic system, and this system will never run out of money. It can never go into liquidation, it can never be made bankrupt, because God is the source not just the supply. This system is available for every child of God. As born-again Christians, we need to realize that we are in the world but not of it. Jesus said,

"They are not of the world, just as I am not of the world."
(John 17:16)

If the children of God were to follow the scriptural principles laid down by God, they would flow in abundance. There would be no shortage of finance to spread the gospel, to fully support ministries, nor to build or buy buildings for the Lord's work, places of worship, Christian schools and so on.

The easiest way to hinder the flow of the gospel is for the devil to bind our finances. We need no reminder that we fight an "invisible" enemy. Yet praise God we have the power to break his hold.

"For we do not wrestle against flesh and blood, but against principalities, against powers, against the rulers of the darkness of this age, against spiritual hosts of wickedness in the heavenly places."

(Ephesians 6:12)

It would be no good walking down the main street of a war zone with a bow and arrow, if the enemy was fighting with top-of-the-range weapons. In war, we must meet like with like. If Satan is warring against our finances, then we must fight back with financial weapons. We fight by giving God back what is rightfully His – His tithe – and by making our offerings. Remember God's tithe is not an offering!

It really is possible under God's instruction and direction, to give your way out of debt!

> *"Therefore submit to God. Resist the devil and he will flee from you."*
>
> (James 4:7)

As you hand your finances over to God, and go on in your giving, your cash flow will increase. Your giving will break the power of debt over your life and the devil must flee. The assignment he has against your finances will be broken. I have personally amplified James 4:7 to read, "Therefore submit to God financially. Resist the devil financially and he will flee from you financially." Your money, when submitted to God is a powerful weapon. Remember our enemy is spiritual.

> *"For though we walk in the flesh, we do not war according to the flesh. For the weapons of our warfare are not carnal but mighty in God for pulling down strongholds."*
>
> (2 Corinthians 10:3-4)

Money is Being Manipulated

There are already powerful groups of people around the world manipulating money, which ultimately will lead to the world's economy being controlled by the anti-christ, the man of sin, the son of perdition. We are about to see the launch of a new monetary system that will eventually replace cash, and the technology used in the very last days will be adapted and used by the anti-christ to control every man, woman and child.

"For God has put it into their hearts to fulfill His purpose, to be of one mind, and to give their kingdom to the beast, until the words of God are fulfilled."

(Revelation 17:17)

The Lord is indeed coming back soon, therefore we must have an understanding of the times we are living in. We must also continually remind ourselves, lest we should forget, that the gospel must be made known to all corners of the earth.

"And this gospel of the kingdom will be preached in all the world as a witness to all the nations, and then the end will come."

(Matthew 24:14)

To fulfill the statement in this scripture I believe, is the most costly operation ever embarked upon throughout world history. It will take billions and billions of dollars. The money is all around the world, it is on planet earth, just waiting to be released by Father. Now is the time for the wealth transfer to be activated. The sooner the gospel is preached around the world, the sooner the Lord Jesus can take us home, and His and our enemy will be dealt with. I repeat, the time for us to activate the wealth transfer is now.

Just exactly how near are we to the cash-less society? The signs would all seem to suggest that we are very near. Recent headlines in newspapers in London state, "The card that is a step closer to the cash-less society."

"Smartcards dispense with cash." A recent television advertising campaign clearly stated that VISA makes cash a thing of the past. If you consider just how many cash transactions can now be handled through the use of a plastic card, you will see just how fast this transition and changeover is taking place. In England at the time of writing in 1998, plastic cards can be used instead of cash in telephone boxes, car parks, petrol pumps, coffee and tea dispensing machines, and various ticket machines. Even parking meters are being replaced with pay and displays points that will accept plastic cards. Many small shops are closing down as a result of the larger stores positioning themselves under "one roof" in malls and out of town locations. All the new stores now have fibre optics installed which will enable the electronic cash transactions to take place.

Your "switch" card is in place of the traditional paper cheque. This facility then enables your account to be debited directly and immediately at the point of sale. Processing cash is an expensive procedure. The banking industry are very keen to introduce far more electronic cash transactions. This would then enable them to decrease their level of staffing, and thereby greatly increase profitability. Automation is bringing redundancy in its wake.

Television banking is now available in various places around the world. The first Internet Bank is already operational in the USA. The functions of both of these avenues is to deal totally with electronic cash transactions. The National Westminster Bank are currently running tests in Cambridge, England with television banking.

The USA's first Internet bank went public on Thursday 23rd May 1996. The Security First Network Bank only have direct deposit arrangement facilities available. Any customers who wish to deposit cheques must do their transactions through the post, rather than the obvious way, which would mean personally going into their local branch. It remains to be seen how quickly consumers will embrace electronic commerce.

The Cash-less Card

What exactly is a "cash-less" card?

The most familiar cards that people in England will have heard about are the "Mondex" card operated through The National Westminster Bank and The Midland Bank, and the "Visa" cash card which I understand is expected to be released soon. Since the middle of 1995 the "Mondex" card has been tested in the town of Swindon, in the south-west of England. More recently the card has been tested in the Universities of Exeter and York. It looks just like a normal bank card, but contains a computer chip in the top left-hand corner. This chip enables transactions to take place, in the same way that electronic data is stored. As you present your "Mondex" card at retail outlets, the purchase value of your goods is deducted from the monetary value stored "in" your micro-chip on the card. To re-load your card you can either use the facility of the cash dispenser machine (A.T.M. Machine) or a especially adapted BT telephone giving you access to the bank's electronic data. You would then after access, key in a personal security code, followed by the amount of cash transfer you needed. This is not a credit facility, you can only transfer funds that you actually have.

Mondex Wallet

The Mondex wallet is a portable device, very similar to a mobile telephone in size and shape, that enables cash to be transferred between cards. This wallet has two slots, top and bottom for the Mondex card to be placed in. Then following the instructions, you can transfer monies from one card to another. The wallet can also give you an up-to-date balance, plus a note of your last ten transactions. It can also store cash within the wallet, giving you the option to transfer cash directly into a bank account.

Mondex Balance Reader

The balance reader looks like, and is the same size as, the electronic device that fits on a key-ring to open car doors without the use of a key. It has a small window on the front, and a slot on the side. You place your card into the slot, and your current balance is clearly displayed in the window. How will this mode of banking affect me? As far as banks and retailers are concerned the effect will be very gradual. We will have the option of either using cash, or one of the above plastic cards available. We will need godly wisdom and understanding for the times we are in. Eventually the technology of this system will lead directly to the financial system, which will ultimately be introduced and controlled by the anti-christ. Brothers and sisters, we are in the last of the last days.

NatWest Bank have just announced "Swindon trial ends 31st July 1998. The fast changing technology that allowed us to launch Mondex in Swindon has now moved on, and the trial must end in readiness for further UK developments."

Now is the time to be radical with our giving to the gospel of Jesus Christ. What will eventually come from this "new technology" will be the system that will enable the mark of the beast to be put into place: the 666 system. That is how very near I believe we are to Jesus returning for His bride. Most children of God in the fellowships that I have ministered in, believe as I do, that they will be part of the rapture.

"For the Lord Himself will descend from heaven with a shout, with the voice of an archangel, and with the trumpet of God. And the dead in Christ will rise first. Then we who are alive and remain shall be caught up together with them in the clouds to meet the Lord in the air. And thus we shall always be with the Lord. Therefore comfort one another with these words."

(1 Thessalonians 4:16-18)

"Then two men will be in the field: one will be taken and the other left. Two women will be grinding at the mill: one will be taken the other left. Watch therefore, for you do not know what hour your Lord is coming."

(Matthew 24:40-42)

Many of you may be thinking or perhaps even hoping, "the mark of the beast, and all that it involves could never happen - 666 is just fictional." Child of God, I assure you that it is very real, and will indeed come to pass. The word of God decrees that it will. It is part of the end-days plan. Some animals in parts of the EEC have already had micro-chips inserted just under their skin by veterinarians, so that a record of that particular animal and breed can be kept. Then when information, or identification of ownership may be required, the animal can just be scanned with a hand-held scanner.

How long will it be before it is socially acceptable to have the chip embedded into your hand? We could then be advised that this would be the easiest and most secure way to "carry" all our personal information with us. Social security numbers, national health numbers, passport information, driving license numbers, bank card numbers, etc., all together and easily accessible, and secure! Most of all, we would plausibly be told, this would be the obvious system to stop theft and fraud. The charge method at the bank or the retail store, or proof of identification would then simply be just a matter of passing your hand over a scanner for fool-proof identification and payment of goods. I want to reassure every one at this point that no-one will be forced to take this mark. I personally believe that this mark will be optional until after the rapture. Then those who are left behind and who truly then recognize that Jesus is Lord will have to decide their own fate by their choice of either accepting or refusing the mark. Hence the vital necessity to finance the gospel so that millions of people will hear the good news and commit their lives to the Lord now. These types of cards would appear to be an excellent way to conduct your financial affairs. Let me make it quite clear **these cards are not the mark of the beast**, they are just the beginnings of the technology that will finally introduce personal micro-chip identification.

It is perfectly acceptable to use these cards with their micro-chip, but clearly we must **never** have the chip injected into our hand or forehead. This mark is obviously connected with the ability to purchase goods and transfer cash payments, as we do now in our present banking system. Ultimately the acceptance of this mark will in the very last of the last days clearly show who is for the beast and who is against him.

"He causes all, both small and great, rich and poor, free and slave, to receive a mark on their right hand or on their foreheads, and that no one may buy or sell except one who has the mark or the name of the beast, or the number of his name. Here is wisdom. Let him who has understanding calculate the number of the beast, for it is the number of a man: His number is 666."

(Revelation 13:16-18)

The Greek word for "mark" is charagma (khar'-ag-mah); a scratch or to cut into, an etching, i.e. stamp as a badge of servitude (Strong's 5480/5482).

We as Christians will be in no doubt as to who the anti-christ is when he does emerge. He will be a man who will be very charismatic, powerful, a political figure who will appear to have the solutions to many world problems.

Because of the continuing problem of stolen credit cards, there is on-going research into "fail-safe" ways of making our credit cards and our pin code numbers theft proof. National identity cards are very much in the news at the moment. I was very interested to read a newsletter from the Royal Bank of Scotland to their Access card holders. The following is an extract from that letter:

BEYOND 2000

"With ever advancing technology it is possible that in the future there will be fewer cheques and cash and much more plastic. With an embedded micro-chip, a personal plastic card could become much more than a credit card. It could be our personal banker, our passport, our driving license, our wedding license, our school, our health, and our job records and dare we say it our birth and our death certificates. And it doesn't have to be the same size or shape as a credit card. With miniaturization it might be built into a watch or a ring that only worked when worn by its owner. Or maybe an implant – the mind boggles. Another interesting development is that at a recent pop concert in Kuala Lumpur starring the group "BOYZONE" the only way that 2,200 people could gain access to this private concert was to purchase a "Swatch Access" Watch. An advertisement in The Star dated 22nd August 1997 for the "Swatch Access" says that "with this watch you can store data, instead of carrying money. Access technology lets you store pre-paid credit to access everything from museums to meals. Transport to entertainment, and much more" - all at the flick of a wrist!"

> *"So the first went and poured out his bowl upon the earth, and a foul and loathsome sore came upon the men who had the mark of the beast and those who worshiped his image."*

> (Revelation 16:2)

The American Standard Version says "a malignant sore." Not sores but just one single sore. Could this be the result of continuous scanning of an imbedded micro-chip causing a skin cancer, or possibly leakage from a tiny lithium battery that actually powers the chip? This micro-chip is called a bio-chip and is a transponder which can be injected just under the skin surface. It is the size of a grain of raw rice. These chips can be tracked from a satellite six miles high and can be located to within a distance of one square metre. Reports of a recent study conducted in the USA apparently concluded that the parts of the body most sensitive to temperature change, which could be used to generate tiny amounts of power (enough to run a micro-scopic battery in an identification chip), are located on the forehead, and on the back of the hand!

Can you now see how desperate it is that the church of Jesus Christ come into order with their tithes and their offerings? This is the only thing that will break the devil's hold on our personal finance, and ultimately on the church corporately. Jesus has forewarned us that in the end days there will be those who try to deceive us.

"And Jesus answered and said to them: 'Take heed that no one deceives you.'"

(Matthew 24:4)

*   *   *   *

As I reflect in the year 2005 on this revised chapter of my book, we can see that the move towards the cashless society is in progress. So much commerce is now being conducted over the internet, and in the banking systems, and "direct debit" is being used more and more.

In December of 2001 it was announced in the media that the "VERICHIP has arrived, a revolution in the making." The VERICHIP is now available. It is a miniaturized and implantable device for Personal Identification, it is the size of a single grain of rice. Each chip has a verification number, and can be used ultimately to provide personal related information.

As it is implantable, it cannot be stolen, lost, or even counterfeited. Through a simple injection process the chip can be implanted just under the skin, once injected this chip can then be scanned with a compatible scanner.

The focus of this chip is not only in the security arena, but in the financial arena also. Credit cards, direct debit authorizations, and other banking facilities could all be incorporated in this tiny transponder. This transponder emits a small amount of radio frequency when activated by a proprietary VERICHIP reader.

To tighten security measures at some borders, finger-printing has already been introduced. How long will it be before the "chip" will be in every day use ? It is time to sit up, and take notice ! There are very clear signs that the worlds economy is being manipulated, this manipulation is ultimately to bring into place that which the apostle John saw, and is recorded in the book of Revelation.

"He causes all, both small and great, rich and poor, free and slave, to receive a mark on their right hand or on their foreheads, and that no one may buy or sell except one who has the mark or the name of the beast, or the number of his name."

(Rev 13: 16-17)

The spirit of anti-christ is preparing its power base, and the implantable micro-chip is now available. Eventually the "chip" will be used in all financial transactions we need to make. It will be recommended as a replacement to our plastic cards. World security is in jeopardy, and terrorism is on the increase. One day, and be assured that this day will come, personal identification will be required for everyone.

Chapter 3

Kingdom Economics

God has placed within His word, a system, that when fully operational by us, allows us to move and flow into complete abundance, even where there has previously been lack. To flow in total abundance we will need complete and continued obedience to His word, and accurate administration of God's tithe. The fact that tithing is systematic does **not** mean that it is legalistic.

Tithe = 10%

Firstly we need to understand that the tithe belongs to God. It is not ours, and must be returned to God. The tithe is an expression of gratitude to God by His people. Tithing is our acknowledgement of God's ownership of everything in the earth. As we know, the tithe is 10 percent of our total financial income. This includes all the things I have already listed, even redundancy payments. In fact any financial increase whatsoever that comes into your life. Once you have returned the tithe to father God He will then be able to open the windows of Heaven over your life.

The only thing that opens the windows of heaven is God's hand. This He does, in obedience to the church returning His tithe. The figures that have been widely quoted in the past about the church of Jesus Christ tithing, is that only 20 percent of the church world-wide tithe regularly and accurately. This presumably leaves 80 percent that do not tithe, or tithe when they feel that they can afford it! If you can literally imagine God opening a window to pour down blessings on us, yet as He opens it He knows He can only open it 20 percent, through our disobedience. This must mean that 80 percent of our corporate blessings are still being held up! Individual tithers are of course blessed, 100 percent, but corporately, as one body, if we do not tithe, we are stemming the flow of blessings across the body.

> *"When He had been baptized, Jesus came up immediately from the water; and behold, the heavens were opened to Him, and He saw the Spirit of God descending like a dove and alighting upon Him."*
>
> (Matthew 3:16)

On the day of Jesus' baptism, Father God opened the windows of Heaven over His son, and Jesus was then empowered with the Holy Spirit. We know from the word of God, that all that Jesus did was blessed. This was because He ministered with authority under a totally open heaven.

> *"'Bring all the tithes into the storehouse, that there may be food in My house, and try Me now in this,' says the LORD of hosts, 'If I will not open for you the windows of heaven and pour out for you such blessing that there will not be room enough to receive it.'"*
>
> (Malachi 3:10)

Here God gives us His word that He will indeed open the windows of Heaven and pour out so much blessing. Can you imagine? God is willing to pour out "so much blessing" that He himself says "we will not have room enough to contain it." These blessings are not necessarily always financial, but we are assured that He Himself will rebuke the devourer over our lives. The list of blessings therefore becomes endless, when the devourer is rebuked. Our families, our children, our health, our jobs, our homes, our finances, and on and on. He will also ensure that our vine will not cast its fruit. These then are the blessings that are ours, and they come when we return to God His tithe. Remember that the tithe is **not** an offering. It is **not** something that you are giving to God. It is something that you are, and **should be returning**.

The offering is separate from the tithe. It has a different function and carries different promises. It is what God measures our increase and our return on. As we make our financial offerings to God, He then gives us back more, so that we can then put more back into the work of God. It is "God perpetuating." God has put a system into operation, that can never fail regardless of the state of the world's economy. This system is based on seed time and harvest.

> *"While the earth remains, Seed time and harvest, cold and heat, winter and summer, and day and night shall not cease."*
>
> (Genesis 8:22)

To fully understand Kingdom Economics will need a complete renewing of the mind and a change of understanding. The measure of your understanding is the measure in which you receive, when you fully move into operating God's Kingdom Economics.

> *"Happy is the man who finds wisdom, and the man who gains understanding."*
>
> (Proverbs 3:13)

> *"And do not be conformed to this world, but be transformed by the renewing of your mind, that you may prove what is that good and acceptable and perfect will of God."*
>
> (Romans 12:2)

Kingdom Economics is a process, not a get rich quick plan. It is simply developing a financial relationship with Father. After all, we give the Lord our hearts, our lives, our families, our health our homes and our jobs, so why not our finance? Satan has blinded the body of Christ for 2,000 years about finance, and about our financial inheritance. Now is the time for the greatest financial release into the body of Christ that the world has ever seen. This is to finance and fulfill the great commission. But it must be done the right way scripturally, God's way. The exciting thing is that you can be part of the releasing mechanism. God is looking for, and preparing stewards for the wealth transfer.

"My people are destroyed for lack of knowledge..."
(Hosea 4:6a)

Please do not let your lack of biblical financial knowledge destroy your life, your vision or your ministry.

The laws of harvest work on the same principles as agricultural laws. If you plant financial seeds into the kingdom of God you will receive a financial harvest.

"But this I say: He who sows sparingly will also reap sparingly and he who sows bountifully will also reap bountifully."
(2 Corinthians 9:6)

The measure in which you give to God, determines the measure that God can release back to you.

"But others fell on good ground and yielded a crop: some a hundredfold, some sixty, some thirty."
(Matthew 13:8)

I think it is good to remind ourselves as more and more money is needed to finance the gospel, running ministries, building new churches, purchasing buildings, expanding Christian television globally, it is not our responsibility to raise money for the Kingdom of God, but it is our responsibility to release it. It is far easier to release money than to raise it. Raising money requires physical action, releasing money requires spiritual authority. Can you see the difference? God has made provision for a tremendous release of wealth to finance His plans, and you can be a part of stewarding this wealth transfer.

"Though he heaps up silver like dust and piles of clothing like clay. He may pile it up but the just will wear it, and the innocent will divide the silver."

(Job 27:16-17)

Chapter 4

Things Unseen

So often we look in "the natural" at our earthly circumstances. We feel that we cannot give to God because we are in debt, or because we need to pay bills. We may also need a holiday, or something new for the home. The thing that keeps a business financially healthy is cash flow, and cash flow in the Kingdom of God will keep your own finances healthy. God will not release us more finance, until we give Him what we already have. Money may leave your hand, but it will never leave your life. When you give money to the Kingdom of God it leaves your present, but enters immediately into your future. Your future need is in your present seed.

"He who observes the wind will not sow, and he who regards the clouds will not reap."

(Ecclesiastes 11:4)

As an example, if you had a hairdryer that you plugged in to the power supply, but did not switch on, you would just have a useless piece of plastic in your hand. However, as soon as you turned on the power, that which was lifeless would be energized. As Christians we have a power source, the Holy Spirit. You, your ministry, or your church, has the power to break the financial restraints that may be holding you back from God's plans for your life.

"While we do not look at the things which are seen, but at the things which are not seen. For the things which are seen are temporary, but the things which are not seen are eternal."

(2 Corinthians 4:18)

Begin now to superimpose the spiritual on to the physical.

I hear many Christians speaking out negative confessions about their finance. "I never have enough money, I will always be in debt, I will never pay off any of my mortgage." These are negative statements. Jesus cannot work on negative statements. Only on positives. Jesus is the high priest of our positive confession. The devil can use our negative words to try and prevent our financial breakthrough. Speak positively, and prophetically to your future. "I will always have an abundance that I may bless others. I am going to come out of debt, my mortgage will be paid off, earlier than the time previously agreed." Take time to speak positively about your financial situation. Most millionaires have been heard to say at some point in their life "I am going to be a millionaire," and then they went on to achieve that goal.

Do you really know the destructive power that wrong words can have, in gossip, or lies, or even curses? There really is life or death in the tongue. Positive words are creative, negative words are destructive. Let us remember that God created the world by His words. "Let there be": light, water, an expanse called sky, the seas...

When I was in the business world, I earned a good salary, drove a company car, and had an expense account. All seemed well, but really I was trusting in my own right arm, and rarely asked God for anything. If I needed something I just got it myself! I also had a substantial amount of savings to fall back on should a problem ever arise. I never thought about seeking God for financial increase, that I could then sow back into the Kingdom of God. It just never occurred to me.

"Ask and it will be given to you; seek and you will find; Knock and it will be opened unto you. For everyone who ask receives, and he who seeks finds, and to him who knocks it will be opened."

(Matthew 7:7-8)

Set your mind on financial increase. But also set your mind on what you want the increase for.

"But seek first the Kingdom of God and His righteousness, and all these things will be added to you."

(Matthew 6:33)

There are many millions of people who need to receive Jesus Christ as their Lord and Saviour. This will take billions of dollars to finance. I believe that we are the end-time generation that God is going to use to finance this final great harvest of souls.

Brothers and sisters, God wants to bless you with abundance, so that you can give out of abundance. Jesus is not coming back for a poverty-ridden church, but for a glorious and prosperous church, without spot or blemish.

"Therefore beloved looking forward to these things, be diligent to be found by Him in peace, without spot and blameless."

(2 Peter 3:14)

Money will be Worthless

During the tribulation, inflation will become so bad that even precious metals will lose their value. There will be no point in hoarding up gold, silver, or gem stones. There will be no security in doing so.

"Throw away your money! Toss it out like worthless rubbish, for it will have no value in that day of wrath. It will never satisfy nor feed you, for your love of money is the reason for your sin. I gave you gold to use in the decorating of your temple, and you used it instead to make idols! Therefore I will take it all away from you. I will give it to foreigners and to wicked men as booty. They shall defile my temple. I will not look when they defile it, nor will I stop them. Like robbers, they will loot the treasures and leave the temple in ruins."

(Ezekiel 7:19-20, Living Bible)

What is God teaching us about money in these last days? We can see that since the last world war, England has been prospering. In the seventies and in the early eighties money was flowing freely. If we think back to our own life-styles at that time, money seemed to flow more liberally. How much of our income actually went into financing the gospel or blessing others, who perhaps were not as well off as ourselves? Admittedly years ago there was not much teaching on finance or giving, therefore, through lack of knowledge we did nothing.

"Get wisdom! get understanding! do not forget, nor turn away from the words of my mouth."

(Proverbs 4:5)

God is speaking to His people about money. The world recession has stopped us in our tracks, and our attitudes are changing. The church of Jesus Christ has the ability to change the world economy before the final collapse, when money will become worthless!

"Come now you rich, weep, and howl for your miseries that are coming upon you. Your riches are corrupted, and your garments are moth-eaten. Your gold and silver are corroded, and their corrosion will be a witness against you and will eat your flesh like fire. You have heaped up treasure in the last days."

(James 5:1-3)

I believe that we have a short period of time to activate the wealth transfer, and for the body of Christ to get themselves into right financial order.

> *"Now the multitude of those who believed were of one heart and one soul; neither did anyone say that any of the things that he possessed were his own. But they had all things in common and with great power the apostles gave witness to the resurrection of the Lord Jesus. And great grace was upon them all. Nor was their any among them who lacked: for all who were possessors of land or houses sold them and brought the proceeds of the things that were sold and laid them at the apostles feet, and they distributed to each as anyone had need."*

(Acts 4:32-35)

In keeping to God's principle they had no lack. How much do we want see what was recorded in the book of Acts, happening in our churches today – the act of giving one to another? Jesus said, "It is more blessed to give than to receive," which shows us that as we give to the body of Christ it will bind us together, it will create unity, and will release God's blessing in greater measure. Yet we cannot "give" if we don't "have."

> *"I have shown you in every way, by labouring like this, that you must support the weak. And remember the words of the Lord Jesus, that He said, 'It is more blessed to give than to receive.'"*

(Acts 20:35)

Satan wants to keep the body of Christ in a position of lack, poverty, and debt. This is totally contrary to the word of God. There is a fierce spiritual battle going on. We must understand the terms of war-fare, so that we can start to corporately go on the offensive, making us totally victorious.

Satan is not fighting us, he is just trying to defend the territory that he is losing! We need to remember that he is just a fallen angel.

"How you are fallen from heaven, O Lucifer, son of the morning!"

(Isaiah 14:12)

The body of Christ are on the offensive, Satan and his army are on the defensive. Satan wants to hinder all that God would do in our lives. If we allow him to be successful, he could possibly stop all the blessings that God has assigned to us, and for us.

Chapter 5

The Root of the Problem

In this chapter, I want to share a revelation that the Father has shown me. I believe that this revelation is a major key to the unlocking of the heavens, and to revival in the church. When God wants to use us, the first thing He looks for is our trustworthiness, not our talent. When God asks you to do something, please do not focus on any risks that may be involved, just focus on the rewards. God is a reward-based God.

> *"But without faith it is impossible to please Him, for he who comes to God must believe that He is, and that He is a rewarder of those who diligently seek Him."*
>
> (Hebrews 11:5-6)

All that He asks us to do will bear fruit, but remember that most fruit is 'out on a limb.'

The enemy is not just after your provision, he is after your PURPOSE. The authority you have in Christ outranks your natural ability, for *we are a victorious people. We are more than conquerors; we are the head and NOT the tail.* The only way to a place of authority is through faithfulness, when you take action you take control!

The Word of God tells us that Satan is an *"evil genius"* (John 14:30 *The Amplified Bible*). He is persistent, but not victorious.

Jesus is THE Victor. He is our Winner. He is our Champion, and He is THE Conqueror. We need to pinpoint exactly where Satan first contended for man's authority and blessings. Yes, you are right, it all started in the garden. This was the entry point he used. We have to understand why he is still able to operate in the same way now, as he did then, despite us being in a new and better covenant.

> *"Now the serpent was more cunning than any beast of the field which the LORD God had made. And he said to the woman, 'Has God indeed said, "You shall not eat of every tree of the garden?"'"*
>
> (Genesis 3:1-2)

After "the fall," the stewardship roll between man and God was broken. Satan had waited for Eve to be created, so that two could come into agreement of disobedience.

When God told Adam *"not to eat of the tree of knowledge of good and evil,"* Eve had not yet been created.

> *"And the LORD God commanded the man, saying, 'Of every tree of the garden you may freely eat; but of the tree of the knowledge of good and evil you shall not eat, for in the day that you eat of it you shall surely die.' And the LORD God said, 'It is not good that man should be alone; I will make him a helper comparable to him.'"*
>
> (Genesis 2:16-18)

> *"And the LORD God caused a deep sleep to fall on Adam, and he slept; and He took one of his ribs, and closed up the flesh in its place. Then the rib which the LORD God had taken from man He made into a woman, and He brought her to the man."*
>
> (Genesis 2:21-22)

41

The problem in the garden was not that Eve was tempted, it was that her husband Adam did not take up his position as high priest of the house. He simply disobeyed God by coming into agreement with Eve, completely disregarding what God had already told him. From that point on, they were both literally outside the garden, and their disobedience ultimately gave Satan the title rights to the world's wealth (see Luke 4:5-6).

Jesus restored this authority through His death and resurrection on the cross. It wasn't until a spirit of generosity was released into the early Christian church, as shown in Acts 2:44-47, that people began *"sharing in all things"* with each other. The blessings and the goodness of God was clearly evident in their lives.

> *"Now the multitude of those who believed were of one heart and one soul; neither did anyone say that any of the things he possessed was his own, but they had all things in common. And with great power the apostles gave witness to the resurrection of the Lord Jesus. And great grace was upon them all. Nor was there anyone among them who lacked; for all who were possessors of lands or houses sold them, and brought the proceeds of the things that were sold, and laid them at the apostles' feet; and they distributed to each as anyone had need."*
> (Acts 4:32-35)

People were selling their land and houses, and laying the proceeds of these sales at the apostles' feet. This generosity was not man manipulated, but Holy Spirit inspired. The apostolic is being released back into the church, demonstrating a clear sign that there is a link between the apostolic anointing and financial release, and ultimately "wealth transfer."

The early church was experiencing abundance, which obviously was a big problem for Satan. He then began to formulate a plan to stop, or at least to change, this "abundance."

He saw his opportunity to thwart our abundance when Ananias, with Sapphira, lied in the presence of the Holy Spirit. This lie caused their death. The fact that they withheld an offering was one thing, and entirely up to them. What killed them was lying to the Holy Spirit!

> *"But a certain man named Ananias, with Sapphira his wife, sold a possession. And he kept back part of the proceeds, his wife also being aware of it, and brought a certain part and laid it at the apostles' feet. But Peter said, 'Ananias, why has Satan filled your heart* **to lie to the Holy Spirit** *and keep back part of the price of the land for yourself?'"*
>
> (Acts 5:1-3)

We can see after this incident, the radical giving of the saints had stopped. And there is no further account of radical giving, or abundance from Acts 5 to the end of Revelation, except in the Macedonian church which at that time gave out of lack.

> *"Moreover, brethren, we make known to you the grace of God bestowed on the churches of Macedonia: that in a great trial of affliction the abundance of their joy and their deep poverty abounded in the riches of their liberality. For I bear witness that according to their ability, yes, and beyond their ability, they were freely willing."*
>
> (2 Corinthians 8:1-3)

What happened at the time was that a withholding spirit was released into the foundation and the DNA of the newly established Christian church. Now we must ask ourselves the question, "Why is this spirit still operating in the church today?" What authority does this withholding spirit have to still operate within the church fabric? The answer is obvious and very simple. The body of Christ has given this spirit the power to operate by feeding it the very thing it was released to do – to withhold! We are "feeding" it through ignorance or disobedience, but we are feeding it.

Let me explain. Offerings we give because the money is ours to give. The tithe we do NOT *give*. This is something we *return*. The fact that we return it (Malachi 3:7) means it was never ours in the first place. By NOT returning the Father's tithe, we are withholding it. Saints, if we corporately return Father's tithe, the power and the authority of the withholding spirit will be broken down, and we will all then be under an open heaven. If only 20 percent of the church tithes, then the windows of heaven are closed 80 percent. Sadly, it is that simple. Can you imagine what would happen in a fellowship when 100 percent of the people were to return Father's tithe to Him? Under an open heaven, there would be souls saved, miracles taking place, healings manifested, and marriages made whole. In fact, we will receive all that is rightfully ours – total blessings – through an open heaven anointing.

The Lord has shown me how to conduct effective and safe spiritual warfare on the issue of the withholding spirit, thereby releasing an open heaven. The withholding spirit is a principality, and I believe it is the highest demonic power under Satan himself.

In the spirit realm, there is position and also rank structure. The position of this principality is to govern and command demonic powers that are under it.

> *"For we do not wrestle against flesh and blood, but against principalities, against powers, against the rulers of the darkness of this age, against spiritual hosts of wickedness in the heavenly places."*
>
> (Ephesians 6:12-13)

There are four very clear levels of demonic rulership. The demonic powers that accompany the "withholding" principality are: lack, poverty, debt, insufficiency, stinginess, bankruptcy, robbery, meanness, fear of giving, and probably more! As I have previously shared, we must start to starve this spirit, and its accompanying demonic powers by NOT withholding. Starvation is far more effective than raising our voices.

Does Satan have a kingdom? Yes, for the Bible says, *"If Satan casts out Satan, he is divided against himself. How then will his kingdom stand?"* (Matthew 12:26). Does Satan have an army? Yes. As I have already shared, there are *"principalities, powers, rulers of the darkness of this age, and spiritual hosts of wickedness."* Although it seems that Satan is continually attacking the body of Christ, in reality, he is trying desperately hard to keep the territories he is losing. As he continues to defend, we must continue to attack so that the Kingdom of God advances.

Before we look at the heavens and their structures, may I emphasize at this point that any decisions we make in obedience to what God has requested, will always attract a certain amount of spiritual warfare from the enemy's camp. If Satan can influence your mind or decisions, he can potentially influence the direction of your life. This could ultimately lead you unwittingly into disobedience.

> *"And do not be conformed to this world, but be transformed by the renewing of your mind, that you may prove what is that good and acceptable and perfect will of God.... For the weapons of our warfare are not carnal but mighty in God for pulling down strongholds, casting down arguments and every high thing that exalts itself against the knowledge of God, bringing every thought into captivity to the obedience of Christ, and being ready to punish all disobedience when your obedience is fulfilled."*

(Romans 12:1-2; 2 Corinthians 10:4-6)

Chapter 6

The Three Heavens

God has instituted spiritual laws. These laws are not the laws of the Old Testament, as they have been fulfilled. These spiritual laws have been set to govern and protect our kingdom. Every law has a penalty if it is violated. For example, there is the law of gravity ("a force that tends to draw all bodies towards the centre of the earth" – *Collins Dictionary*). No matter how many times we jump from a building, believing in faith we would not fall to the ground, the law of gravity would very quickly come into force because a physical law has been broken. In the same way, when we break or violate spiritual laws, which ultimately are God's ordinances for our lives, Satan has legal authority to enforce penalties. This is why, in God's love and mercy – and for our protection – He calls His people to lead **blameless** and **obedient** lives.

> *"When Abram was ninety-nine years old, the LORD appeared to Abram and said to him, 'I am Almighty God; walk before Me and be **blameless**.'"*
>
> (Genesis 17:1)

> *"If you are willing and **obedient**, you shall eat the good of the land."*
>
> (Isaiah 1:19)

"...but as He who called you is holy, you also be holy in all your conduct, because it is written, 'Be holy, for I am holy.'"

(1 Peter 1:15-16)

Let us now look at what is going on in the structure of the heavenlies. There are **three** heavens, Satan is only the prince of the power of the air, and not the earth!

*"And you He made alive, who were dead in trespasses and sins, in which you once walked according to the course of this world, according to **the prince of the power of the air**, the spirit who now works in the sons of disobedience."*

(Ephesians 2:1-3)

Satan can only affect what is happening on earth by deceiving and manipulating human behaviour, the mood, and the manner of society. God owns the earth, and the title rights to the world's wealth is now, potentially, under our authority.

"'The silver is Mine, and the gold is Mine,' says the LORD of hosts."

(Haggai 2:8-9)

"The earth is the Lord's, and all its fullness, the world and those who dwell therein."

(Psalm 24:1)

"The heaven, even the heavens, are the Lord's; but the earth He has given to the children of men."

(Psalm 115:16)

Satan does NOT OWN THE WORLD... nor does he have legal rights to it. Also, because God's people have not legally challenged Satan, he is in fact trespassing on our property!

"In the beginning God created the heavens and the earth."

(Genesis 1:1)

Here, we see clearly defined that the word "heavens" is plural, and "earth" is singular.

There are **three heavens**. The first heaven is the earth and the atmosphere. The second heaven is the spirit realm above the earth and the atmosphere. The third heaven is the abode of God.

The Scriptural confirmation of the **second heaven** is:

*"How you are fallen from heaven, O Lucifer, son of the morning! How you are cut down to the ground, you who weakened the nations! For you have said in your heart: 'I will ascend into heaven, I will exalt my throne above the stars of God; I will also sit on the mount of the congregation on the farthest sides of the north; I will ascend **above the heights of the clouds**, I will be like the Most High.'"*

(Isaiah 14:12 -14)

The Scriptural confirmation of the **third heaven** is:

*"I know a man in Christ who fourteen years ago – whether in the body I do not know, or whether out of the body I do not know, God knows – such a one was caught up **to the third heaven**. And I know such a man – whether in the body or out of the body I do not know, God knows."*

(2 Corinthians 12:2-3)

Logically, if there is a second heaven and a third heaven, then there must be a first heaven.

The "principalities and powers" are a very organized and structured demonic force. I believe that they operate from the second heaven, and it is from this heaven that they try to control what is happening on earth.

> *"For we do not wrestle against flesh and blood, but against principalities, against powers, against the rulers of the darkness of this age, against spiritual hosts of wickedness in the heavenly places."*
>
> (Ephesians 6:12)

Now that we have established that there are three heavens, I want to share on the power of the withholding spirit, and its place in the second heaven. To "withhold" means *"to hold back, to restrain, to keep from giving."* This spiritual force, in the second heaven works in two ways. It can hold back blessings coming down from the third heaven, the abode of God, and it can also hold back our prayers, intercession, praise and worship going up from the earth. This is why it is so important that we have a clear passage; in fact, an "open heaven" to God.

The Importance of an Open Heaven

These powers and principalities in the second heaven have full authority to hold back our blessings. This authority is fully theirs by our acts of disobedience. Because the tithe is Father's and belongs to Him (and not us), when we choose not to tithe, we are deliberately withholding from God! When we return our tithes to Father, the withholding spirit is broken over our lives. Can you imagine all the blessings that can then flow down from God to us? In the same way, if the church of Jesus Christ all returned Father's tithe to Him, I believe that corporately across the earth the church would just explode into a glorious revival. Think about it. If not one person holds back from God that which is rightfully His, the power and the authority of that spirit would be broken! All the powers controlled by it would also be fragmented, and there would be no authority to even form a withholding barrier!

The latest figures I have, state that 80 percent of God's people are not returning the tithe. This means that the windows of heaven are, and can only be, opened 20 percent. As an individual regular and accurate tither, the windows of heaven are open 100 percent over your life, but NOT corporately over the body of Christ. This is why we are not seeing all that God has promised happen in our churches – His continued blessings. We seem to concentrate so much on what we can do to get things happening, instead of focussing strongly on WHY things *are not* happening! Disobedience is a free-will choice, but we cannot choose the consequences that follow our disobedience.

> *"...and what is the exceeding greatness of His power toward us who believe, according to the working of His mighty power which He worked in Christ when He raised Him from the dead and seated Him at His right hand in the heavenly places, far above all principality and power and might and dominion, and every name that is named, not only in this age but also in that which is to come. And He put all things under His feet, and gave Him to be head over all things to the church, which is His body, the fullness of Him who fills all in all."*
>
> (Ephesians 1:19-23)

Rejoice that Jesus is indeed at the right hand of the Father, and is above ALL things!

Chapter 7

Radical Giving

"And I also say to you that you are Peter, and on this Rock I will build my church and the gates of hell shall not prevail against it and I will give you the keys of the Kingdom of Heaven, and whatever you bind on earth will be bound in Heaven, and whatever you loose on earth will be loosed in Heaven."

(Matthew 16:18-19)

This is a very powerful scripture for binding powers and principalities. Look carefully at where Jesus says *"whatever you bind on earth, will be bound in Heaven, and whatever you loose on earth will be loosed in Heaven."* "Whatever," actually means whatever! Therefore we must assume this binding to include our monies. We have ourselves probably unintentionally "bound" up our finance in banks, building societies, or investments. It seems possible that we can "bind up" the supernatural flow of money from Heaven.

God is calling His church to become radical in their giving, so that the wealth transfer can be activated. Passive or stingy offerings will not loose God's end-time financial resources. Our giving is not only an act of worship to the Father, but it is also a positive war action against the devil. Passivity never won a battle!

51

"And from the days of John the Baptist until now the Kingdom of Heaven suffers violence, and the violent take it by force."

(Matthew 11:12)

We trust God for most things; our salvation, which is the gift of eternal life, for healing, for deliverance, for our job situation, for our families, for our future. When it comes to **our** money that is something quite different. It seems that finance, is an area where some of us still only trust ourselves, and our "own right arm" to work things out for us.

For His end-time church Father wants us to totally trust Him. There is no security at all in earthly things.

"Do not lay up for yourselves treasure on earth, where moth and rust destroy, and where thieves break in and steal: but lay up for yourselves treasure in Heaven, where neither moth nor rust destroy, and where thieves do not break in and steal."

(Matthew 6:19-20)

We enter the world with nothing, and we leave the world with nothing. You just cannot take your money with you, it's impossible. The wealth of the world stays behind, on planet earth and is recycled. Have you ever thought about that – I mean really thought about it? After all, Jesus said "But lay up for yourselves **treasure in Heaven**." When you actually release your money where God has told you to by His Holy Spirit, you are in fact depositing your money in spiritual credit form. This deposit is two-fold, because it is also for your future withdrawal when you need it. Remember, your future need is in your present seed.

When God asks us to give, there is always a blessing. Obedience commands a blessing. God always wants to encourage us. Radical giving is a powerful force, and is honoured by God. I know personally, that it moves financial barriers that may be around us, or our ministries.

> *"There was a certain man in Caesarea called Cornelius, a centurion of what was called the Italian Regiment, a devout man and one who feared God with all his household, who gave alms generously to the people, and prayed to God always. About the ninth hour of the day he saw clearly in a vision an angel of God coming in and saying to him, 'Cornelius!' And when he observed him, he was afraid, and said, 'What is it, lord?' So he said to him, 'Your prayers and your alms have come up for a memorial before God.'"*

> (Acts 10:1-4)

Here is an example of one man whose giving was noticed by God because he was devout, God-fearing, gave generously to those in need, and prayed regularly.

When Jesus was sitting opposite the treasury watching the people making their offerings, it was a poor widow that He noticed on that particular day. Not because of the amount that she gave but because that which she gave was her **all**. It was a radical action. The widow had no other money, that was it, she gave out of poverty, rather than abundance. They were her last two mites, in fact we are told it was her "whole livelihood" This particular act of giving is still remembered today.

> *"Now Jesus sat opposite the treasury and saw how the people put money into the treasury. And many who were rich put in much. Then one poor widow came and threw in two mites, which make a quadrans. So He called His disciples to Himself and said to them, 'Assuredly, I say to you that this poor widow has put in more than all those who have given to the treasury; for they all put in out of their abundance, but she out of her poverty put in all that she had, her whole livelihood.'"*

> (Mark 12:41-44)

53

Here is another account of radical giving.

"Then Mary took a pound of very costly oil of spikenard, anointed the feet of Jesus, and wiped His feet with her hair. And the house was filled with the fragrance of oil."
(John 12:3)

Jesus was so blessed with Mary's prophetic and generous action that He then prophesied that the gesture would be known wherever the gospel was preached world-wide.

"Assuredly, I say to you, wherever this gospel is preached in the whole world, what this woman has done will also be told as a memorial to her."
(Mark 14:9)

Here we read two examples of offerings, very different in size, but both radical! Brothers and sisters please do not think that if you have little money, that God is not happy with your offering, or that God cannot use you financially. That is a **lie** of the devil. It is interesting to note the act of giving that God wanted recorded in His word, was the radical action of two woman. It is not what we give, but what is left after our giving, that the Lord sees.

God can start to use you even if you are in debt. Giving to God can bring you out of debt. The action that will destroy the spirit of debt over your life is radical giving. The Father delights in your offering. Satan cannot stand the action of offerings to the Father. In fact scripture tells us that the very first murder was committed over an offering. Cain murdered his brother Abel, because Abel's offering was more pleasing to God than Cain's.

"And in the process of time it came to pass that Cain brought an offering of the fruit of the ground to the LORD. Abel also brought of the firstborn of his flock and of their fat. And the LORD respected Abel and his offering, but He did not respect Cain and his offering. And Cain was very angry, and his countenance fell. So the LORD said to Cain, 'Why are you angry? And why has your countenance fallen? If you do well, will you not be accepted? And if you do not do well, sin lies at the door. And its desire is for you, but you should rule over it.' Now Cain talked with Abel his brother; and it came to pass, when they were in the field, that Cain rose up against Abel his brother and killed him."

(Genesis 4:3-8)

Our corporate level of giving is not high enough to break the stronghold that powers and principalities have on the end-time financial provision that God has set aside for His church. Church, please stop trying to raise money for the Kingdom of God, and start releasing it. Raising money in the world has a cut-off point, but releasing money from Heaven does not. We are all waiting for God to move financially in our lives, yet He is waiting for us to move. Without God we cannot, without us, God will not. Radical giving **will** release a radical response from Heaven.

Chapter 8

The Wealth Transfer

Satan took by deception, the title rights of the world's wealth from Adam, until the death and victorious resurrection of the Lord Jesus Christ. Now they are ours in and through Jesus. But what are we, the church of Jesus Christ doing about taking back and re-establishing ownership of the wealth of the world?

> *"Then the devil, taking Him up on a high mountain, showed Him all the kingdoms of the world in a moment of time. And the devil said to Him; All this authority will I give you, and their glory, for this has been delivered to me, and I give it to whomever I wish. Therefore, if you will worship before me, all will be yours."*

> (Luke 4:5-6)

The first point I would like to bring out here is that Satan was only tempting Jesus with something that ultimately Jesus was going to inherit anyway, through the cross and resurrection. Remember Satan never gives you anything. God's word tells us,

> *"The thief does not come except to steal, and to kill, and to destroy. I have come that they may have life, and that they may have it more abundantly."*

> (John 10:10)

The second point is that immediately after Satan spoke, Jesus rebuked him straight away, saying,

"Get behind me Satan! for it is written you shall worship the Lord your God, and Him only shall you serve."
(Luke 4:8)

Note, Jesus never corrected Satan on the statement he made about giving Jesus the wealth of the world.

"...All this authority will I give you, and their glory, for this has been delivered to me."
(Luke 4:6)

That is because this authority was "delivered" to Satan in the Garden of Eden, but now in and through the wonderful victorious name of Jesus we have the authority over the world's wealth.

"And Jesus came and spoke to them, saying, 'All authority has been given to Me in heaven and on earth.'"
(Matthew 28:18)

Now through the cross we have power over debt, lack, poverty, insufficiency, and mammon. All these things are broken and defeated powers. Obedience is the only key to walking in this authority. Giving releases victory in the spiritual realm, against that which would delay the wealth transfer. The word of God says,

"The wealth of the sinner is stored up for the righteous."
(Proverbs 13:22)

The term "sinner" usually refers to those who consciously make a lifestyle of sin, rather than the righteous who occasionally fall into sin.

The "righteous" are the church of Jesus Christ, but is the church of Jesus Christ righteous enough to receive this wealth transfer? God is bound by His own word. He will not transfer the wealth from an unrighteous world to an unrighteous church.

If the wealth were transferred in this present day, how would we use it? How much would go to the spreading of the gospel of Jesus Christ? Would there be unity in decision-making? Is there integrity in the people who would steward such a transfer? The amounts would be enormous! Is our book-keeping solid enough to stand up to inspection by say, the Tax Office, or the Charity Commissioners? Satan would love to bring the church into disrepute with a financial scandal. So we must ask ourselves are we really ready for this wealth transfer? God is looking for good stewards.

> *"One who increases his possessions by usury and extortion gathers it for him who will pity the poor."*
>
> (Proverbs 28:8)

When was the last time we thought about the poor, or when did we last bless the poor? Are our business dealings honest? Do we as Christian business men pay our staff a fair wage? Are we totally honest with company expenses? Do we make the correct returns to our Inland Revenue or government taxation offices?

> *"Therefore submit yourselves to every ordinance of man for the Lord's sake..."*
>
> (1 Peter 2:13a)

God has given us the keys to release finance into our lives so that we are able to finance the end-time harvest and to be a blessing to others.

> *"For God gives wisdom and knowledge and joy to a man who is good in His sight; But to the sinner He gives the work of gathering and collecting, that He may give to him who is good before God..."*
>
> (Ecclesiastes 2:26a)

"Though He heaps up silver like dust and piles up clothing like clay, he may pile it up, but the just will wear it, and the innocent will divide the silver."

(Job 27:16-17)

The outpouring of the Holy Spirit truly leads me to believe that we are now in God's special time slot for the final wealth transfer to take place.

Later in this book I will be looking at the principles of tithing in greater depth, but at this stage I would like to inform you that those, who do not or will not tithe, do not qualify for the wealth transfer.

Father wants His servants to prosper in each and every area of their lives.

"Let them shout for joy and be glad, who favour my righteous cause; and let them say continually 'Let the Lord be magnified, who has pleasure in the prosperity of His servant.'"

(Psalm 35:27)

The gift of prosperity is not a "Bless Me" gift. It is a gift to enable you to bless others, and to finance the work of the living God. That is what the final wealth transfer is all about. Please determine in your own heart that you will become prosperous, so that you can be a blessing to the body of Christ.

Chapter 9

Operational Financial Authority

Once we have made a commitment to the Lord and have become born-again, we have moved ourselves spiritually into another Kingdom. This is what is referred to when the Lord says,

> *"They are not of the world, just as I am not of the world."*

(John 17:16)

We now serve a new master, and follow different principles. The administration of our finance now also comes under this new Kingdom principle. The god of the "world," Satan, corrupts and manipulates the world's financial system, but he does **not** own the wealth within that system. Please grasp, and put into action the fact that God clearly tells us,

> *"And you shall remember the LORD your God, for it is He who gives you power to get wealth, that He may establish His covenant which He swore to your fathers, as it is this day."*

(Deuteronomy 8:18)

The power that we have been given through salvation is to release money by spiritual means rather than to raise it by physical means. The world's financial system is opposed to the Kingdom of God. Only when we operate God's system in total

60

obedience will it enable us to finance the end-time harvest and retrieve that which is rightfully ours. The definition of authority is the power or right to do something – particularly to give orders and to see that they are followed. The word "authority" as used in the Bible usually means a person's right to do certain things because of the position or office he or she holds. The word emphasizes the legality and the right, more than the physical strength, needed to do something.

"And Jesus came and spoke to them, saying, 'All authority has been given to Me in heaven and on earth.'"

(Matthew 28:18)

All authority belongs to the Lord. Yet He has clearly told us in Luke 10 that we can overcome all the power of the enemy by the authority He has given us. In the word we see that Jesus acknowledged Satan's power, but re-assures us that through Him we have the victory.

*"And He said to them, 'I saw Satan fall like lightning from heaven. **Behold, I give you the authority to trample on serpents and scorpions, and over all the power of the enemy, and nothing shall by any means hurt you.**'"*

(Luke 10:18-19)

It is not our authority that overcomes the enemy, but the authority that Jesus has given us. When you have received the baptism of the Holy Spirit, which is confirmed by speaking in a heavenly language (see Acts 2:4), you have been empowered from on high to receive that power and authority.

"But you shall receive power when the Holy Spirit comes upon you, and you shall be witnesses to me in Jerusalem and in all Judea and Samaria, and to the end of the earth."

(Acts 1:8)

Please understand that many born-again spirit-filled Christians who have been empowered by the Holy Spirit are not exercising this authority. Consequently, they do not see breakthrough in many areas. Here are two examples of the Lord encouraging us to use all that He has made available for us.

1.   *"When the day was now far spent, His disciples came to Him and said, 'This is a deserted place, and already the hour is late. Send them away, that they may go into the surrounding country and villages and buy themselves bread; for they have nothing to eat.' But He answered and said to them, 'You give them something to eat.' And they said to Him, 'Shall we go and buy two hundred denarii worth of bread and give them something to eat?' But He said to them, 'How many loaves do you have? Go and see.' And when they found out they said, 'Five, and two fish.' Then He commanded them to make them all sit down in groups on the green grass. So they sat down in ranks, in hundreds and in fifties. And when He had taken the five loaves and the two fish, He looked up to heaven, blessed and broke the loaves, and gave them to His disciples to set before them; and the two fish He divided among them all. So they all ate and were filled. And they took up twelve baskets full of fragments and of the fish. Now those who had eaten the loaves were about five thousand men."*

(Mark 6:35-44)

In verse 37 Jesus was giving the power and authority to the disciples, to perform a miracle of provision. The disciples did not understand what Jesus meant by the statement "you give them something to eat." They assumed He meant for them to buy food, but what He really meant was literally, "you give them something to eat." Jesus was telling them that they have the power and the authority to activate a creative miracle.

2.   *"Now in the fourth watch of the night Jesus went to them, walking on the sea. And when the disciples saw Him walking on the sea, they were troubled, saying, 'It is a ghost!' And they cried out for fear. But immediately Jesus spoke to them, saying, 'Be of good cheer! It is I; do not be afraid.' And Peter answered Him and said, 'Lord, if it is You, command me to come to You on the water.' So He said, 'Come.' And when Peter had come down out of the boat, he walked on the water to go to Jesus. But when he saw that the wind was boisterous, he was afraid; and beginning to sink he cried out, saying, 'Lord, save me!' And immediately Jesus stretched out His hand and caught him, and said to him, 'O you of little faith, why did you doubt?' And when they got into the boat, the wind ceased."*

(Matthew 14:25-32)

In verse 29 Jesus was giving the power and authority to Peter to defy the forces of gravity. The first step for Peter to activate this authority was to actually make a conscious decision to get out of the boat. This authority allowed him to walk in the power that could defy gravity. It was only lost when he took His eyes off Jesus. He looked down, and supposedly thought "I do not have the power to do this," and then he just began to sink. As doubt enters authority leaves. Brothers and sisters, you have this authority available to you in the financial realm when you return your tithes and give your offerings. Never ever doubt or harden your hearts to the financial promises that God has made to you. The only way to a place of financial authority is through financial faithfulness.

Chapter 10

Breaking the Chains of Mammon

The god of this world is money: mammon. It is the thing which motivates and controls most of the people on earth. God says,

"You shall have no other gods before Me."

(Exodus 20:3)

But who is stewarding the wealth of the world? At present the money is in crime syndicates, drug cartels, pornography, prostitution, the Mafia, and the triads. Other large money-spinners are alcohol, tobacco, gambling and the rock music industry. There will soon be a great "shaking" of the world, the like of which has never been seen before. God will show the world that all the silver and all the gold is His.

"For thus says the LORD of hosts: 'Once more (it is a little while) I will shake heaven and earth, the sea and dry land; and I will shake all nations, and they shall come to the Desire of All Nations, and I will fill this temple with glory,' says the LORD of hosts. 'The silver is Mine, and the gold is Mine,' says the LORD of hosts. 'The glory of this latter temple shall be greater than the former,' says the LORD of hosts. 'And in this place I will give peace,' says the LORD of hosts."

(Haggai 2:6-9)

If you commit to financially put God first before your bank and savings accounts, and before your nest-eggs, things will start to happen in your life! Things that will change your life so completely, that you will honestly wonder why you didn't "step out" sooner. You will have a greater peace, a far deeper relationship with the Father, and increase in your finances. This change brings a change of lifestyle, but more important, it brings a change of heart.

> *"For the love of money is the root of all kinds of evil, for which some have strayed from the faith in their greediness, and pierced themselves through with many sorrows."*
>
> (1 Timothy 6:10)

You don't even have to have money to love it. The continual thought of how you can acquire it, can become a dangerous and unhealthy desire. There is nothing wrong with us having money, what is wrong is if money has us!

The wealth transfer is going to happen. There will be a dramatic impact on the world, when the Church of Jesus Christ holds the world's wealth. The devil is a counterfeiter, so at the moment he is releasing many financial distractions. One of these distractions is the lottery. The God we serve is not a God of chance. Nor do I believe that as Christians we should be purchasing lottery tickets.

> *"Wealth not earned, but won in haste, or unjustly, or from the production of things for vain or detrimental use such riches will dwindle away. But he who gathers little by little will increase his riches."*
>
> (Proverbs 13:11, Amplified)

As Christians we cannot, and must not, rely on the world's financial system. We must look to Jesus.

"No one can serve two masters; for either he will hate the one and love the other, or else he will be loyal to the one and despise the other. You cannot serve God and mammon."

(Matthew 6:24)

Chapter 11

Supernatural Supply

Brothers and sisters, God will always supply finance for His work, and His workers. But there are spiritual principles that have to be obeyed. How could we possibly finance what needs to be financed in these last days through our own efforts? God has made a promise to us, a covenant promise, which is absolutely "Satan-proof."

> *"And you shall remember the Lord your God, for it is He who gives you the power to get wealth, that He may establish His covenant which He swore to your Fathers, as it is this day."*
>
> (Deuteronomy 8:18)

We are empowered!

The power to get wealth is not necessarily you earning that wealth, it is the power of the Holy Spirit's anointing, to release it to you, and through you.

Vast amounts of money are needed to spread the gospel to all corners of the earth, before the return of the Lord Jesus. The promises that the Lord made with Abraham apply to us today. Abraham was a very wealthy man. How many of us are as blessed as Abraham was? Most of us know the chorus "Abraham's blessings are mine" but are we seeing those blessings in our lives? They need to be appropriated through obedience to the word.

God will start to reveal where the treasures are, as we come into the place of obedience with our tithing and giving. We will then receive revelation about end-time finance. Do you own your own land? Then begin to prophesy over your land for riches to come forth. Ezekiel prophesied over dry bones and they sprang into life. Speak to your bank accounts, prophetically, and with authority saying "Finance come forth." Do not think that that is too radical. We are in the last days and we need to be radical to enable us to push the boundaries of the natural, into the realm of the supernatural. Radical action from us will cause radical action from God. If you want God to do something in your life He has never done before, then you do something for God that you have never done before, radically give!

"I will give you treasures of darkness and hidden riches of secret places, that you may know that I the Lord, who call you by name, am the God of Israel."

(Isaiah 45:3)

In November 1997 the British media announced that gold had been found in the west of England. I feel that this find has an end-days significance.

As I wrote this chapter I felt an excitement come over me, culminating in the following word from the Lord.

"Come into place my people, come into place, for that which I have is about to be released, come into place so I can release my resources to you. Resources of abundance. I will shake the heaven and the earth, and the sea and the dry land. The world will see My power and My glory. All the silver and all the gold is mine, and I will give it to whom I wish. Come into place My church and receive that which I have for you."

Please take time in quietness to meditate upon this word. The church corporately cannot bring a solution to its financial condition until we make a correction as to how we steward God's money.

Honour the Lord

"Coming into place" means that we must honour God with our money. When we honour God in this way, we are also trusting **Him** with a very important part of our lives, our security. Even if it appears that we cannot afford to tithe, God will never let us down, if we honour **Him** with what is rightfully His, His tithe. The "tithe" is 10 percent of all of our income. When you set aside God's 10 percent, God will then bless your 90 percent. It is really very simple – you just cannot afford not to tithe.

The Tithe

Father is speaking very directly to His church, about the return of His tithe. Please put aside all your religious and theological reasoning. Please especially lay aside a much used misnomer that "tithing is Old Testament." We all know who started that rumour, *"the one who is a liar, and the father of lies"* (John 8:44). I will deal with exactly why tithing is not Old Testament further on.

The Correct Placement of the Tithe

> *"Bring all the tithe into the storehouse that there may be food in my house."*
>
> (Malachi 3:10a)

There seem to be many discussion points as to where we can place, send, or give our tithe. Let me show you in the word of God exactly where I believe the tithe should regularly be returned.

> *"You must tithe all of your crops every year. Bring this tithe to eat before the Lord your God at the place he shall choose as **his sanctuary**. This applies to your tithes of grain, new wine, olive oil, and the firstborn of your flocks and herds. The purpose of tithing is to teach you always to put God first in your lives."*
>
> (Deuteronomy 14:22-23 Living)

We clearly see from this scripture that the tithe does in fact go into the house of God. I personally believe that the tithe should go into the church where you are spiritually fed, where you are a member, where you are committed and where you are pastored. I am sure that at this point many of you will be saying "but I give 10 percent of my salary to an itinerant ministry or to some deserving charity." But may I confirm again, that the tithe belongs to your own church. Malachi says "bring," not "send." Anything else that you feel the Lord wants you to support, is an offering above and separate from the tithe, and remember the Lord gives us our **increase** on our offerings. According to the word of God He will always supply seed.

"Now may He who supplies seed to the sower, and bread for food, supply and multiply the seed you have sown and increase the fruits of your righteousness."

(2 Corinthians 9:10)

It is right for us to walk honourably before the Lord, but this walk must also include honouring Him in all aspects of our finance.

"For those who honour me I will honour."

(1 Samuel 2:30)

When we honour God by returning His tithe to Him, we should be sure we understand exactly what we are tithing on.

"The first of the first fruits of your land you shall bring into the house of the Lord your God."

(Exodus 23:19a)

The "first fruits" of our salaries means that we tithe on gross and not on net. That means that we honour God before the tax man! If not, we are still robbing God on the amount that the tax office deduct. Our tithing must be accurate. Spiritually it is vital that the right amount is deducted. There are two reasons why: one is that there is a monetary difference between gross and net, and secondly that the differing amount is something that the enemy could use as a loop-hole.

> *"'And I will rebuke the devourer for your sakes, so that he will not destroy the fruit of your ground, nor shall the vine fail to bear fruit for you in the field,' says the LORD of hosts."*
>
> (Malachi 3:11)

God's heart is to bless you, and to prosper you, but we must be obedient to God's word regarding finance. Nothing releases God's blessing faster, nor in greater abundance than obedience.

> *"Beloved I pray that you may prosper in all things and be in health, just as your soul prospers."*
>
> (3 John 2)

Yes, God wants to prosper your life here on earth, but our prosperity must align with the word of God.

Biblical prophecy is being fulfilled almost daily. Jesus is returning soon. The finance that God gives us, we should use to spread the gospel, bless others, and also give in obedience by the prompting of the Holy Spirit where He directs. By doing this, God will release back to us in greater measure, so that we in turn can increase our giving into the Kingdom.

> *"But seek first the Kingdom of God and His righteousness, and all these things shall be added to you."*
>
> (Matthew 6:33)

When we are stewards of God's wealth we can enjoy all the benefits of God's household. If you are a trusted servant or steward you will be like Joseph, who owned nothing but had everything.

> *"Let them shout for joy and be glad, who favor my righteous cause; and let them say continually, 'Let the LORD be magnified, who has pleasure in the prosperity of His servant.'"*

(Psalm 35:27)

Chapter 12

Your Financial Release is in the Word of God

"Happy is the man who finds wisdom, and the man who gains understanding."

(Proverbs 3:13)

Kingdom economics are for us to understand how to release money. Please stop trying to raise finance for the Kingdom and start releasing it. It is far easier to release than to raise!

"Get wisdom! Get understanding! Do not forget, nor turn away from the words of my mouth."

(Proverbs 4:5)

Solomon was a very radical giver. He was also very wise, and with this wisdom came great wealth.

Buildings Released to Christians

Before Jesus returns, God wants His Kingdom on earth expanded. How many people does your church hold? Could you believe God for a new building that would hold 10,000 people? A building, that if God wanted it to, would incorporate a book shop, a coffee lounge, counselling suites, leisure facilities, and even all the equipment for a video ministry within the church complex. God stirred up King Cyrus to build a temple at Jerusalem, and God then released the money to him.

"Thus says the Lord to His anointed, To Cyrus whose right hand I have held – To subdue nations before him. And to loose the armour of Kings, To open before him the double doors, so that the gates will not be shut: I will go before you and make the crooked places straight: I will break in pieces the gates of bronze and cut the bars of iron. I will give you the treasures of darkness and hidden riches of secret places, that you may know that I am the Lord, who calls you by name, I am the God of Israel."

(Isaiah 45:3)

"Thus says Cyrus King of Persia all the kingdoms of the earth the Lord God of Heaven has given me, and He has commanded me to build Him a house at Jerusalem which is in Judah."

(Ezra 1:2)

The final great harvest of souls cannot be financed by a crumbling world economy. God has set aside the wealth of the world for His plans, and He has given us the power to release it.

"And you shall remember the Lord your God, for it is He who gives you the power to get wealth, that He may establish His covenant which He swore to your fathers as it is this day."

(Deuteronomy 8:18)

God's covenant promise is still the same, yesterday, today, and forever.

"Forever, O LORD, your word is settled in heaven. your faithfulness endures to all generations; you established the earth, and it abides."

(Psalm 119:89-90)

We have been, and are, empowered to attract wealth individually, and corporately. The covenant promises are Satan-proof. But we need to move firmly into position to claim them.

The Key to God's Unlimited Blessing for You

This section that I am about to share with you now, is the very heart-beat of the book that I have been commissioned by Father to write. The revelation that Father has given **me**, will be life-changing for **you**. I really want you to understand that your blessings, decreed to you by God through Abraham are far too often locked up in the spirit realm. They need to be released. What we do on earth does affect what is happening in the spirit realm.

Remember,

"For we do not wrestle against flesh and blood, but against principalities, against powers, against the rulers of the darkness of this age, against spiritual hosts of wickedness in the heavenly places."

(Ephesians 6:12)

God's word cannot be changed, adapted, or modified just to suit us. God has breathed, by His spirit into men, His word to be recorded for ever. He can only act on His own words.

"He who is faithful in what is least, is faithful also in much; and he who is unjust in what is least is unjust also in what is much. Therefore if you have not been faithful in the unrighteous mammon, who will commit to your trust the true riches? And if you have not been faithful in what is another man's, who will give you what is your own?"

(Luke 16:10-12)

This scripture could apply to God's tithe. For example *"not being faithful in what belongs to another."* If we cannot be trusted to return 10 percent of what God has released to us, how can God trust us with greater wealth? Would you trust someone with vast sums of your money, if that person never paid you back what he owed you? Probably not!

> *"No servant can serve two masters, for either he will hate the one and love the other, or else he will be loyal to one, and despise the other. You cannot serve God and mammon."*

(Luke 16:13)

The Tithe

The definition of "tithe":

Tithe = a tenth part, to pay a tithe of one's income etc. (Collins Dictionary)

What I am going to share with you about "the tithe" has literally changed the lives of thousands of people. When God called me out of the business world. He gave me one very clear mandate, "Go out into the world and tell my people to stop robbing me." This completely counteracts the lie that Satan has perpetuated for years, that tithing is Old Testament! Returning the tithe to God enables Him to totally fulfill His continued covenant promise of blessings to us. One way that the covenant promise of blessings can be broken, is by man's disobedience to God in not returning the tithe.

We are all one. The corporate body of Christ is made up in people parts. Therefore if one part of the body is not functioning, it obviously affects the other parts. This means that non-tithers must obviously affect the other parts of the body. They may be totally unaware of it, and it is probably unintentional, but nevertheless it is true, they are affecting the corporate church as a whole. However, individual tithers will not have their blessings blocked, but corporately we are affected.

I want at this stage to build for you a strong foundation about the tithe, and bring about a great and mighty change in your life. This change will lead you into the fullness of all that God has for you. We will now look at all that the prophet Malachi spoke about regarding the tithe, the wealth transfer, and the coming of the Lord Jesus Christ.

The only way that God can open the windows of Heaven and release blessings to us, is when we obediently and consistently tithe. These blessings cannot be stopped by any demonic power. Whatever your position is at this moment in time, you may be a millionaire, you may have no money at all, or you may be deep in debt, I can say from my own personal experience, and also from the hundreds of testimonies that reach my office, that the Lord will bless you as you tithe. The Lord commits by His word to bless you; in fact He encourages you to try it!

> *"'Bring all the tithes into the storehouse, that there may be food in My house, and try Me now in this,' says the LORD of hosts, 'If I will not open for you the windows of heaven and pour out for you such blessing that there will not be room enough to receive it.'"*
>
> (Malachi 3:10)

This is the one and only scripture where God challenges us to test him. **Please remember the testimonies that you read at the beginning of this book.** Please do not think that you cannot afford to tithe. I would like to assure you that you can afford to tithe, whatever your circumstances. Because the Lord requires the firstfruits of our monies,

"Honour the Lord with your possessions, and with the firstfruits of all your increase."

(Proverbs 3:9)

Please remember this is before tax.

I have compiled the following listings to help those who aren't sure exactly what to tithe on:

- Any financial harvest that comes in after your seed sowing. 10% of this harvest is still God's, even though you have sown for it. The 90% left on that particular increase is still for you to steward.
- **Businesses** - If you are in business and have two accounts, i.e. personal and business, they should both be tithed on. I suggest that on your personal account you tithe as normal, either weekly or monthly. The business account tithe should be calculated and paid at the end of the year on your net profits before corporation tax.
- The other normal things that we may overlook are Bonuses, Inheritances, Child Benefit, Family Allowance, Income Support, Income Tax Refunds, Monetary Gifts, Pensions and Annuities.
- Of course with your salary you start tithing on gross, before tax.
- A loan from a bank, which you are obviously going to pay back, is **not** an increase, therefore no tithe is required.

The fact that tithing is systematic does not make it legalistic. We are simply working in complete accuracy with Father's money. For many years I have always recorded my income, so that I am certain at any given moment in time exactly what the tithe is. In this way even the smallest amount of money is logged. I have shown an example of my record book here.

Income	God's tithe	Myself
$100.00	$10.00	$ 90.00
$174.00	$17.40	$156.60
$ 12.00	$ 1.20	$ 10.80
Total Income $286.00	**The tithe is $28.60**	**$257.40**

It is easy to see that at the last entry made, for **myself** there is $257.40 available. The $28.60 – God's tithe – does not even come into **my** calculations.

When you keep a record of your finances this way you always know exactly how much you have. Everything in the middle column is God's, and God's first fruits always remain available to take to the Storehouse. It is then simply a question of adding up the tithe column.

> *"And all the tithe of the land, whether of the seed of the land or of the fruit of the tree, is the LORD's. It is holy to the LORD."*

(Leviticus 27:30)

Because the tithe is Holy it must be consumed. This means that if we do not return to God His tithe, the enemy has authority to devour that 10%. The accounts that I hear as I travel around the world confirms to me that the enemy always takes far more than the 10% we should have returned. He "takes" in various ways: car repairs, household repairs, unexpected bills that just seem to come from nowhere. The promise from God is, that by returning His tithe, He will rebuke the devourer. Presumably, if we rob God the devourer is not being rebuked. I am sure that you will agree with me, that if you do not tithe, your money just seems to evaporate. There are two options available for God's tithe: we either return it to God, or we allow Satan to devour that same amount, or possibly more.

Just Who Should Tithe?

Tithing is a principle for everyone. Here I am particularly addressing, Ministers, Pastors, Priests, Ministry leaders, and all those in leadership. I am sure as men and women of God that you tithe your personal income, but now I would like to show you scripture that requires that you also tithe out on the ministry income that you receive from your people.

> *"Then the Lord spoke to Moses saying 'Speak thus to the Levites, and say to them: When you take from the children of Israel the tithes which I have given you from them as your inheritance, then you shall offer up a heave offering of it to the Lord a tenth of the tenth.'"*
>
> (Numbers 18:25-26)

You should give your tithe to another ministry which the Holy Spirit leads you to. Please do not block the blessings coming into your ministry by robbing God of His tithe, on the tithes and offerings given into your church, fellowship or ministry. What we do in the physical affects what happens in the spiritual. How can you really expect a financial breakthrough for your ministry if the incoming finance is not being tithed out? You are then returning to God what is His, and acknowledging that He is the financial source of your ministry.

> *"You must tithe all your crops every year. Bring this tithe to eat before the Lord your God at the place that He shall choose as His sanctuary. This applies to your tithes of grain, new wine, olive oil, and the first born of your flocks and herds. The purpose of tithing is to teach you always to put God first in your lives."*
>
> (Deuteronomy 14:22-23, Living Bible)

Teaching on the Tithe

When accurate teaching is brought to your congregation on the tithe, I assure you that the revelation on tithing and giving will be activated into their hearts and spirits. If you do not teach on tithing and giving you are robbing your people of blessings and financial increase.

"For the lips of a priest should keep knowledge and people should seek the law from his mouth, for he is the messenger of the Lord of Hosts."

(Malachi 2:7)

If you have not been tithing your ministry finance out, or not really even brought teaching on the tithe, I suggest that you seek the Lord in repentance, and then immediately start to do both. Once again, I can confirm that you will see an increase in your ministry, in many ways, not just financial. I have numerous testimonies whereby once a Pastor has begun to tithe out on the ministry finance, buildings have been released, numbers have grown, and there has been a greater anointing in all areas within that particular ministry.

"To bring the firstfruits of our dough, our offerings, the fruit from all kinds of trees, the new wine and oil, to the priests, to the storerooms of the house of God; and to bring the tithes of our land to the Levites. For the Levites should receive the tithes in all our farming communities and the priests, the descendants of Aaron shall be with the Levites when the Levites receive tithes; and the Levites shall bring up a tenth of the tithes to the house of our God to the rooms of the storehouse."

(Nehemiah 10:37-38)

If you are part of a ministry that has several branches, your own branch tithe should not go to another branch or to the central office. That is simply keeping it in the family! It should be given to a ministry that is nothing to do with your own group. If there is a ruling or a requirement that 10 percent of the finance is to be given to the central office, then I would suggest to you that it is a levy, or a subscription, rather than a tithe. I cannot see that as meeting God's requirement of the tithe. Do return to the central office the 10 percent levy required of your "group," but step out in faith, and give what is a "tithe", 10 percent, to another ministry where directed by the Holy Spirit. These are God's words, not mine! *"Test me..."*

God has promised that He will open the windows of Heaven over your ministry, and also He will rebuke the devourer. Do not let the devil steal from you any longer.

> *"'Bring all the tithes into the storehouse, that there may be food in My house, and try Me now in this,' says the LORD of hosts, 'If I will not open for you the windows of heaven and pour out for you such blessing that there will not be room enough to receive it. And I will rebuke the devourer for your sakes, so that he will not destroy the fruit of your ground, nor shall the vine fail to bear fruit for you in the field,' says the LORD of hosts."*
>
> (Malachi 3:10-11)

Chapter 13

The First Murder

"And in the process of time it came to pass that Cain brought an offering of the fruit of the ground to the LORD. Abel also brought of the firstborn of his flock and of their fat. And the LORD respected Abel and his offering, but He did not respect Cain and his offering. And Cain was very angry, and his countenance fell."

(Genesis 4:3-5)

I often wondered why God favoured Abel's offering and not Cain's. After all, they both offered from the work of their hands: Cain from the ground and Abel from his flock. I believe the reason behind God's disappointment in Cain's offering is this. God had clearly laid down a pattern for offerings. When we read the account of the fall in the garden of Eden, we see that God clothed Adam and Eve because they now "recognized" that they were naked.

"Also for Adam and his wife the LORD God made tunics of skin, and clothed them."

(Genesis 3:21)

Therefore we must presume that to clothe them with "skins" of innocent animals must have required the shedding of blood. This early foreshadowing of substitutionary atonement firstly points toward the necessity of judgement upon the innocent to provide a "covering" for the guilty. Secondly when Cain saw that his offering did not please God he allowed sin to come into his heart. It manifested as anger, and then anger became murder, and outworked itself in the murder of Abel his own brother. Cain did not follow the pattern laid down by God, he did his own thing, the thing that was easiest for him.

> *"Now Cain talked with Abel his brother, and it came to pass, when they were in the field, that Cain rose up against Abel his brother and killed him."*

(Genesis 4:8)

The word **"anger"** becomes **"danger"** simply by adding a "d."

Satan hates you to make any kind of offerings to God, particularly financial offerings. He will do anything to try and stop you from honouring God with your finance. As we have just read, Satan immediately moved in on Cain through jealousy, leading to hatred, and then subsequently to murder.

Let us now understand why Abel's offering was so pleasing to God. It was because Abel followed the pattern of requirement laid down by God for blood offerings to Him. He gave the first "fruits" of his flock. This was without Abel realizing it, a prophetic action of tithing.

> *"Abel also brought of the firstborn of his flock [the tithe] and of their fat [an offering] and the Lord respected Abel and his offering."*

(Genesis 4:4)

The very first person to tithe was Abram. The first act of tithing took place 430 years **before** the mosaic law was even written. It was then included in the law. The law was put into place to hold the church together until Jesus came. When Jesus returned to the Father, He left the Holy Spirit with us to guide us. The requirement to tithe is still operational, but now we return the tithe under grace, rather than forcibly under the law. Therefore tithing is not only part of the mosaic law it is a timeless covenant of blessings, which makes it not a begrudged legal requirement, but a joyous exercise in faith. Although tithing was part of the Abrahamic life of faith, it was also an integral part of faithful living. Accurate and obedient tithing expresses faith that God is our true source, and to fail to tithe not only robs God, but also dishonours Him.

"Then Melchizedek King of Salem brought out bread and wine; He was the priest of God most high and he blessed him and said, blessed be Abram of God most high, possessor of Heaven and earth, and blessed be God most high, who has delivered your enemies into your hands and he gave him a tithe of all."

(Genesis 14:18-20)

Prior to any legal requirement, Abram responds to Melchizedek's office of King and priest, by generously giving him a tithe of all the spoils gathered from the recent war.

"For this Melchizedek, King of Salem priest of the most high God, who met Abraham returning from the slaughter of the kings and blessed him, to whom also Abraham gave a tenth part of all, first being translated 'King of Righteousness' and then also King of Salem meaning 'King of Peace' without father, without mother, without genealogy, having neither beginning of days nor end of life, but made like the son of God, remains a priest continually."

(Hebrews 7:1-3)

Melchizedek is a type of Christ in his high priest ministry, thus allowing him to receive the tithe. Jesus Christ is our high priest and our King, and must still receive the tithe from us today.

"Here mortal men receive tithes, but there he receives them, of whom it is a witness that he lives."

(Hebrews 7:8)

This verse has been dated by a scholar named Usher (1581-1656) who was a noted authority on dating events that occurred in the Bible. We are told it was written 30-35 years after the death and resurrection of Jesus. Many biblical scholars accept his dating as accurate. Jesus himself endorsed tithing.

"Woe to you, scribes and Pharisees, hypocrites. For you pay the tithe of mint, anise, and cumin and have neglected the weightier matters of the law. Justice and mercy and faith. These you ought to have done, without leaving the others undone."

(Matthew 23:23)

"But woe to you Pharisees for you tithe mint and rue and all manner of herbs, and pass by justice and the love of God. These you ought to have done without leaving the others undone."

(Luke 11:42)

Jesus himself says,

"Do not think that I came to destroy the Law or the prophets. I did not come to destroy but to fulfill."

(Matthew 5:17)

So we can clearly see that the early New Testament church tithed after the death and resurrection of Jesus.

Chapter 14

God's Property is Holy

The word of God recorded in the Bible, is God-breathed unto men. It is Holy, it is called the "Holy" Bible. God's spirit is "Holy." He is called the Holy Spirit. The tithe is also "Holy."

> *"And all the tithe of the land, whether of seed of the land or the fruit of the tree is the Lord's. It is Holy to the Lord."*
>
> (Leviticus 27:30)

The tithe is God's own personal money. It is not ours to do with as we wish. The tenth part of all our cash income, whether gifts, salary, state benefit, or anything that you reap from a previous sown harvest has to be tithed on. It is all God's and has to be returned to Him.

> *"That you shall take some of the first of all the produce of the ground, which you shall bring from the land that the Lord your God is giving you, and put it in a basket and go to the place where the Lord your God chooses to make His name abide."*
>
> (Deuteronomy 26:2)

An Open Heaven

Jacob saw an open Heaven, not because he was righteous but because of God's call and His faithfulness to Abraham. Jacob was the third generation to receive the promises of the Abrahamic covenant. The Lord identified Himself by His previous relationship with Abraham and Isaac.

> *"Also your descendants shall be as the dust of the earth. You shall spread abroad to the West, the East, the North, and the South, and in you and your seed all the families of the earth shall be blessed."*
>
> (Genesis 28:14)

After Jacob had seen an open Heaven, and seen the abundance of what was in Heaven, he fully realized all that God's covenant promises held for him.

> *"Then Jacob made a vow saying "If God will be with me, and keep me in this way that I am going, and give me bread to eat, and clothing to put on, so that I come back to my father's house in peace, then the Lord shall be my God. And this stone which I have set as a pillar shall be God's house, and of all that you give me, I will surely give a tenth to you."*
>
> (Genesis 28:20-22)

The tithe, although found in the later mosaic law, originated with the earliest patriarchs, Abraham and Jacob. Therefore the tithe is part of the Abrahamic covenant, not a part of the covenants of "works."

The tithe is a basic expression of our trust in God. By tithing we show God that we hold no trust in our own money, nor do we think that "our own right arm" can save us from any situation. We trust totally and completely in God's provision. It also shows that we are agreeing to walk trustingly with Him, in our part of His covenant blessings.

The church of Jesus Christ has to be able to operate under a 100 percent open Heaven. If only 20 percent of the church worldwide tithe, it means that 80 percent of the windows of heaven are closed over the church. To receive the corporate anointing and blessing in fullness, we have to be in total unity over the tithe.

> *"Behold how good and how pleasant it is for brethren to dwell together in unity; it is like precious oil upon the head. It is like the dew of Hermon descending upon the mountains of Zion. For there the Lord commands a blessing – life forevermore."*
>
> (Psalm 133:1-3)

This speaks of the anointing being released where there is unity. Verse 3 speaks of the blessings released. If we cannot be trusted to return God's tithe, how can God trust us with the end-time wealth, which He has laid aside for us? Or more importantly His end-time anointing. The devil wants to stop this anointing, because, as we know, it is the anointing that breaks the yoke. Breaking the yoke of "withholding finance" will bring Jesus back for His bride sooner. By robbing God of tithes and offerings, we are robbing ourselves of the corporate anointing. This is exactly what the devil wants us to do. How can he block the anointing? Money!

> *"He who is faithful in what is least is faithful also in much; and he who is unjust in what is least is unjust also in much. Therefore if you have not been faithful in the unrighteous mammon, who will commit to your trust the true riches? And if you have not been faithful in what is another man's, who will give you what is your own?"*
>
> (Luke 16:10-12)

89

If God cannot trust you with unrighteous mammon – money – how can He trust you with true riches, the anointing? It is God's intention that we be stewards of hundreds of thousands – or possibly even millions – of dollars for the Kingdom. Yes, that is what being under an open Heaven can mean.

> *"When He had been baptized, Jesus came up immediately from the water; and behold, the heavens were opened to Him, and He saw the Spirit of God descending like a dove and alighting upon Him."*
>
> (Matthew 3:16)

Jesus ministered under an open Heaven. We have the same Holy Spirit in us, and we need to remember that. Brothers and sisters, the only way that we can open the windows of Heaven corporately over the whole church of Jesus Christ is to return God's tithe back to God. That is all of us, not just some of us. We must now begin to get radical in our giving. If your offering doesn't move you, how can it move God? An example of moving God with an offering is shown in that Abraham was willing to give to God his only beloved, and long-awaited son Isaac, and we all know that Abraham was a blessed man. I would like you to notice here the order in which Abraham did things. I believe this "order" is of a divine nature, and of paramount importance. These three directives from God, will, if followed, establish God's covenant blessings within your lives, and move you into a position of authority that comes with God's covenant.

Covenant*: A will, testament, pact, contract, an agreed upon plan to which both parties **subscribe**.* (Strong's 1242)

While the word may signify an agreement between two parties with each accepting mutual obligations, most often it is a declaration of one person's will. In the Bible, God initiated the whole action, set the conditions, and defined as a decree a

90

declaration of purposes. God covenanted with Noah, Abraham, Moses and Israel. In the New Testament, Jesus ratified by His death on the cross a new Covenant, termed in Hebrews 7:22 "*a better covenant*". The definition of "**subscribe**" is:

1. to promise to contribute money,
2. to give support to, and
3. to sign one's name at the end of a document as an indication of consent.

The Three Parts to Re-establishing the Covenant of Blessings

1. Abram initiated the tithe to King Melchizedek.
   · **The tithe will protect you financially.**
2. God asks for a blameless walk.
   · **Your integrity will position you financially.**
3. God asks for an offering.
   · **The offering will increase you financially.**

So the three things that God requires from us, in **His** order, are to return His tithe, to walk blameless before Him, and to make offerings. It is interesting that the Lord would have us be blameless before we make our offerings! You see man will always accept your offerings, but God may not.

1. The Tithe

> "*Then Melchizedek king of Salem brought out bread and wine; he was the priest of God Most High. And he blessed him and said: 'Blessed be Abram of God Most High, Possessor of heaven and earth; And blessed be God Most High, who has delivered your enemies into your hand.' And he gave him a tithe of all.*"
>
> (Genesis 14:18-20)

Bread and wine speak of covenant. Melchizedek was "*the*"

91

priest of God most High. He was the only priest that also held the title of King. Jesus is also King and Priest and is in the order of Melchizedek. We see here that this covenant continues. The only thing that can break covenant is death. It is and always will be unbroken, because Jesus is alive.

Please disregard any statements about tithing being Old Testament. This covenant was established 430 years before the law was even written. It is unchanging, it always was, and it always will be.

2. A Blameless Walk

> *"When Abram was ninety-nine years old, the LORD appeared to Abram and said to him, 'I am Almighty God; walk before Me and be blameless. And I will make My covenant between Me and you, and will multiply you exceedingly.'"*

(Genesis 17:1-2)

Financial integrity will attract wealth to you. After blamelessness and righteousness, God has covenanted to then multiply exceedingly.

3. Our Offerings

> *"Now it came to pass after these things that God tested Abraham, and said to him, 'Abraham!' And he said, 'Here I am.' And He said, 'Take now your son, your only son Isaac, whom you love, and go to the land of Moriah, and offer him there as a burnt offering on one of the mountains of which I shall tell you.'"*

(Genesis 22:1-2)

When God asked Abraham for an offering, He actually asked Abraham for his son. It was quite clear what God wanted. God called him by name, "Abraham" so we know that it was impossible for Abraham to say "I didn't know you meant me Lord." Then God said "Take now your son, your only son." Again it was quite clear what God was saying, and quite clear what he required of Abraham – his son. Now, God will also tell you when. In the midst of God requiring His offering, He also reminded Abraham that it was his son that he loved, that was required. There was no way that Abraham could deny the clarity of the offering which God desired. High stakes it would seem! Yet the Lord purely wanted to see how much Abraham loved Him, and of course equally important, how much he trusted Him. We learn a tremendous lesson here, by example, that God will indeed provide for you, but you must be obedient to the requirements of the Lord. God's provision is strategically located along the pathway of faithful obedience. God will always make it clear exactly what offering He requires. After having established what you intend to give, you will have peace. Whatever the figure and circumstance, always look for that inner peace before you give.

The covenant was now established by the three actions we have just read. This covenant is available to all God's people:

"And if you are Christ's, then you are Abraham's seed, and heirs according to the promise."

(Galatians 3:29)

"In your seed all the nations of the earth shall be blessed, because you have obeyed My voice."

(Genesis 22:18)

The only proviso to this covenant is obedience to the terms and conditions.

One Master

> *"No servant can serve two masters; for either he will hate the one and love the other, or else he will be loyal to the one and despise the other. You cannot serve God and mammon."*
>
> (Luke 16:13)

Once we fully understand that all we have is God's then there will be no problem in returning to Him that which is His. When God asks us to give, it is then **His** responsibility to return, and increase, so that we are able to give again the next time He asks us. Following the covenant pattern of Abraham will release great blessings into your life, and the lives of those in the body of Christ. Remember the order, first we tithe, then we walk blameless before God, and then we release our offerings.

> *"Give, and it will be given to you: good measure, pressed down, shaken together, and running over will be put into your bosom. For with the same measure that you use, it will be measured back to you."*
>
> (Luke 6:38)

Offering time is not a time of loss, but a time of gain. Your money may leave your hand but it does not leave your life. It comes from your "present" but enters directly into your future.

Chapter 15

The Key to the Wealth Transfer

Proverbs 13:22 tells us that the wealth of the sinner is stored up for the righteous. There are two vital points to note in this scripture:

1. That the sinners wealth is stored up.
2. That this wealth is stored up only for the "righteous."
   God cannot transfer money from an unrighteous world to an unrighteous church. Throughout this book, when I refer to righteousness, I am purely focusing on financial righteousness.

God is bound by His word.

> *"Heaven and earth will pass away, but My words will by no means pass away."*
>
> (Matthew 24:35)

> *"The LORD reigns, He is clothed with majesty; the LORD is clothed, he has girded Himself with strength. Surely the world is established, so that it cannot be moved."*
>
> (Psalm 93:1)

A Prophetic Word for the Last Days

The Prophet Malachi ("My Messenger") came as a reformer, to warn and change the hearts of the people from a serious spiritual decline. Malachi also "formed" a bridge between the Old and the New Testament. This word is vital for the church in the last days.

Chapter 1

This first chapter talks about honouring Father with a pure offering.

> *"'You also say, "Oh, what a weariness!" And you sneer at it,' Says the LORD of hosts. 'And you bring the stolen, the lame, and the sick; Thus you bring an offering! Should I accept this from your hand?' Says the LORD."*
>
> (Malachi 1:13)

The people offered sick, defective, defiled or diseased animals. These offerings were all obviously substandard and they were worthless to their owners. These offerings, then caused and allowed the priests to compromise by receiving them. In effect what the people gave God had no value. The mosaic law laid down that offerings to God should be unblemished.

> *"And he said to Aaron, 'Take for yourself a young bull as a sin offering and a ram as a burnt offering, without blemish, and offer them before the LORD.'"*
>
> (Leviticus 9:2)

As the priest's right was to eat the offering, this meant that through their compromise of accepting sick and defective animals, they in turn had to eat bad meat. Because they had allowed the standard to drop before God, it also dropped before them. So it is today. As men of God in positions of authority – Pastors, Ministers, Vicars, Clerics, Church leaders etc. – compromise on their teaching about tithes and offerings, they are not only robbing the people of blessings and financial increase, but they in turn are eating diseased meat! No money to run their ministry effectively, nor to move into the vision that God has given them. Money should never be the thing that stops **your** ministry expanding. I feel sure, if you actually asked yourself the question, "What is stopping my ministry from expanding?" the answer would be money!

Chapter 2

The second chapter of Malachi brings a rebuke to the priests. Verse 17 shows us that the priests wearied God when they questioned him about evildoers, asking "Where is the God of justice?" God replied,

> *"You have wearied the LORD with your words; yet you say, 'In what way have we wearied him?' In that you say, 'Everyone who does evil is good in the sight of the LORD and He delights in them,' Or, 'Where is the God of justice?'"*

(Malachi 2:17)

How many times have we said "It's not fair," wearying Him. Perhaps we have said "so and so, who is not a Christian has more money than us, has a nicer car, a bigger house, an excellent job, and is always travelling somewhere nice on holiday," and so on and so on. It would appear that evil seems to prosper. Be assured that God never honours evil conduct. Do not speak against the justice of God. God sees all, and rewards according to His agenda and His time-table, not ours. We must realize and understand that both good and evil conduct does not go unnoticed, nor unrecognized. All **will** be judged, God will honour the faithful.

So many Christians are at a stand-still position, by their own actions. They are wondering where their material blessings are. They are all there, just waiting to be released. One of the reasons why blessings can be withheld from the children of God, is that they are "sitting on the fence" in their walk with the Lord. That means that they are obviously not doing the irregularities and dishonest dealings that the world do concerning finance, yet neither are they doing exactly what God says regarding finance. We as Christians just cannot live on prayer alone, we must act on what the word of God says. We must operate God's system. After all God's promises and Abraham's blessings are ours just waiting to be claimed. The Babylon system (Revelation 18), will not stand for ever. It is already showing cracks, and soon will crumble, and collapse. God's system of giving and receiving will never fail. It can only increase in greater measure. The more that we are in obedience to His system, faith and trust in God will always be rewarded.

"Now faith is the substance of things hoped for, the evidence of things not seen."

(Hebrews 11:1)

"But without faith it is impossible to please Him, for he who comes to God must believe that He is, and that He is a rewarder of those who diligently seek Him."

(Hebrews 11:6)

Chapter 3

I would like us now to take a careful look at the third chapter of the book of Malachi. Despite popular opinion this chapter is not specifically about tithing. In fact this chapter instructs, warns, and prepares us, financially. It also speaks about the rapture. The burden on Malachi's heart was to warn the people about God's ordinances and spiritual laws. From the voice of God speaking through Malachi to the voice of John the Baptist, there was a time period of 400 years. During this period there was silence from God. We can see from this "silence" the importance of this prophetic word through Malachi. One would presume that if God spoke, and then never spoke to His people again for over 400 years, the last things He spoke, He meant! This was vital instruction for the New Testament church. As I have shared in a previous chapter, the first act of tithing took place 430 years before the mosaic law was ever written.

The act of tithing crosses the bridge from the Old Testament to the New Testament. The only thing that was "left behind," was the requirement of the law. Tithing then and now comes under grace, as being our very minimum level of honouring God with our finance. It is very simple – we return the tithe to God because it is His, not ours!

Malachi's form of prophecy was unique. He was the only prophet through whom God posed a series of questions and answers. My personal view on this is that God did not want any misunderstanding over this very important word, particularly in two areas, one of honouring God, and two, returning **His** tithe. He wanted this word to be received into our spirit and then to be outworked continually in our relationship with Him.

The Key to Your Blessings

The prophecy that Malachi brought in chapter three is relevant for today, for God's end-time church. This prophecy proclaimed the coming of Jesus, a refining for the five-fold ministry, and a very clear warning about the exposure of sin. It also makes quite clear reference about the "return" of blessings spoken about in Malachi 3. These blessings are being held up by the devil, particularly in the financial area. When we rob God of His tithe, this gives the devil legal access to rob us, and you will find that the devil takes far more than 10 percent. The blessings that God sends to tithers through His open windows of Heaven are numerous, and they come in many ways.

This passage of scripture is vital for breakthrough, both personally and corporately for the body of Christ. For a complete change in your life, the spiritual dynamics of the tithe must be clearly understood. Therefore I have gone through Chapter 3 verse by verse, and I pray that the Holy Spirit gives you clear revelation and understanding.

Chapter 16

Malachi 3

Verse 1

"'Behold, I send My messenger, and he will prepare the way before Me. And the Lord, whom you seek, will suddenly come to His temple, even the Messenger of the covenant, in whom you delight. Behold, He is coming,' says the LORD of Hosts."

The "messenger" referred to here is John the Baptist who was, as we know, sent to prepare the way for the Lord Jesus. Then in this verse there is a prophetic gap of 2,000 years. Malachi then says, *"and the Lord whom you seek, will suddenly come to His temple."* This does not refer to a stone temple – but to us. We are the temple of the Holy Spirit.

"We heard Him say, 'I will destroy this temple that is made with hands, and within three days I will build another made without hands.'"

(Mark 14:58)

"Do you not know that you are the temple of God and that the Spirit of God dwells in you?"

(1 Corinthians 3:16)

Brothers and sisters, this verse refers to the rapture of the church. When Jesus first came to earth, it was not sudden. The prophets foretold about the coming Messiah, and that He would be the Saviour to the world. In fact three "wise" men were even guided by a star to find His exact place of birth in Bethlehem. But here we are told the Lord whom you seek will **suddenly** come:

> *"But of that day and hour no one knows, not even the angels of heaven, but My Father only."*
>
> (Matthew 24:36)

So we clearly see this prophecy is for the end of the age.

Verse 2

> *"But who can endure the day of His coming? And who can stand when He appears? For He is like a refiner's fire and like fuller's soap."*

The first time Jesus came, He came as Saviour. The next time He comes He is coming for His bride. The scripture is right, who indeed *"can endure the day of His coming?"*

Verse 3

> *"He will sit as a refiner and a purifier of silver; He will purify the sons of Levi, and purge them as gold and silver, that they may offer to the LORD an offering in righteousness."*

A refiner or smelter of precious metals would heat up the gold or silver until the dross or scum formed on the surface of molten metal, would rise to the surface. The refiner would then scrape the dross off, leaving the molten metal dross free and pure. The Holy Spirit is doing exactly the same thing in the lives of the church. He is coming upon the church in such power, that He causes things that need addressing in our lives to rise to the surface. These things are being removed to bring us to a place of holiness. The sons of Levi that are referred to, are the "five-fold" ministry. The Lord wants holiness and righteousness from His apostles, prophets, evangelists, pastors and teachers, so that they then in turn can offer the offerings of God's people in absolute righteousness. God has always required that any offering made to Him, must be offered in absolute purity.

"For the time has come for judgement to begin at the house of God; and if it begins with us first, what will be the end of those who do not obey the gospel of God?"

(1 Peter 4:17)

Verse 4

"Then the offering of Judah and Jerusalem will be pleasant to the LORD, as in days of old, as in former years."

God enjoys receiving our offerings. He delights in pure and generous offerings. In scripture we see that the priests and the people became complacent in what they offered, and also in the way that they presented it. In some cases the offerings were blemished. God does not want to receive an offering that is given grudgingly, nor does He want to receive an offering of inferior quality. Our offering must cost us something. If your offering is not important to you, I would suggest that it is not important to God. By this I do not mean the size of your offering. After all the most talked about offering ever, was the two mites from the widow. So I reiterate, our offering should cost us something. Our offerings should be able to stir the very heart of God.

Verse 5

"'And I will come near you for judgement; I will be a swift witness against sorcerers, against adulterers, against perjurers, against those who exploit wage earners and widows and the fatherless, and against those who turn away an alien – because they do not fear Me,' says the LORD of hosts."

God is telling us that He will come near to us by His Holy Spirit. The purpose for this, we are told, is that God will be a swift witness against the charges related above. In fact this swift "witness" has already begun. **Witchcraft** is continually being exposed by our newspapers. **Adultery** is being exposed almost daily – within the Royal family, within government circles, within the police force, in the film and music industry, and regrettably even within the church. **Perjury** – in the last few years we have read of many court cases, where the verdict has been reversed from that of guilty to innocent, and prisoners have been released, because evidence submitted in court-rooms had been falsified. Mass redundancy is now common-place. **Exploiting wage earners** – many people are experiencing injustice in the work place. As so many people are unemployed some employers have seized this opportunity to offer extremely low rates of pay. This is highly immoral. **Against those who turn away an alien** – we are all aware of the injustices that surround immigration, and visas etc. God says that all these things are happening because they do not fear Him.

Verse 6

"For I am the LORD, I do not change; therefore you are not consumed, O sons of Jacob."

This is a warning. God does not change. We have seen what happens when God judges, but He is always faithful to His covenant promises, and He will not abandon His people.

Verse 7

" 'Yet from the days of your fathers you have gone away from My ordinances, and have not kept them. Return to Me, and I will return to you,' says the LORD of hosts."

What is it that God wants returned? Answer, Money! When we return to God that which is His, He will return to us that which is ours. Let us now examine that word. What exactly is ours? It is very simple; everything that is God's is ours. God will return everything that the devil has stolen. The blessings of God covers everything, even to the secret desires of our heart. God is just waiting to release all our blessings to us. They are locked up in the heavenlies, just waiting to be showered down upon us. These windows of Heaven can only be opened over our lives when we are obedient to the word of God, and return to God that which is rightfully His, **His** tithe. Obedience always brings a blessing.

God is saying, return to me what is mine – my money – and stop robbing me. Then I will return to you, all that has been stored up in the heavenlies for you. My Son Jesus now has the title-rights to the world's wealth (Luke 4:5-8), through the finished work at Calvary.

Verse 8

"Will a man rob God? Yet you have robbed Me! But you say, 'In what way have we robbed You?' In tithes and offerings."

God is clearly saying that mankind is robbing Him. That in itself is an awesome statement, yet God then proceeds to tell us that we are robbing Him in not just one area but in two! The definition of "robbery" is "the taking of another's property." Totally different from the definition "to steal" which is "to take another's property slyly." This shows quite clearly that whoever has been robbed did have original ownership of that which he was robbed of. Malachi asks, *"In what way have we robbed You?"* The word **"we"** talks of corporate robbery. This was the church of The Old Testament, and the body of Christ in the New Testament. When we make a conscious decision not to tithe, we are making a conscious decision not to return to God that which belongs to Him. This is shown in verse 7, *"You have gone away from My ordinances"* (an ordinance is a spiritual law). This is not man's law, nor the law of the Old Testament, but it is God's spiritual law that He put into place for all time and for all mankind.

God says we are robbing Him in two areas:

1. the tithe, and
2. the offering.

Please understand the offering is separate from the tithe. When we rob God in these two areas, we are actually robbing Him of praise, and of worship, and the joy of allowing Him to bless and prosper us.

> *"Let them shout for joy and be glad, who favour my righteous cause; and let them say continuously let the Lord be magnified, who has pleasure in the prosperity of His servant."*
>
> (Psalm 35:27)

We were created to worship God, voluntarily, with a free will, and God obviously wants to bless us. Not just with finance, but with all kinds of blessings that will enrich our lives. God has spiritual laws that He cannot and will not go against. He cannot go against His own words. Put yourself in His place for a moment. Would you really want to bless someone who was continually robbing you? If the relationship increases when we give to someone, how much more will our relationship with God increase as we honour Him, with our tithes, and our offerings? One of the meanings of "offering" is "to present for acceptance, or consideration." Man will always accept your offering, but God may not!

"And in the process of time it came to pass that Cain brought an offering of the fruit of the ground to the LORD. Abel also brought of the firstborn of his flock and of their fat. And the LORD respected Abel and his offering, but He did not respect Cain and his offering. And Cain was very angry, and his countenance fell."

(Genesis 4:3-5)

Verse 9

"You are cursed with a curse for you have robbed Me, even this whole nation."

The curse talked of in this verse, is not **the** curse of being under the law. That curse was dealt with at the cross. This is **a** self-imposed curse/penalty that you bring upon yourselves through disobedience to a spiritual law that has been put in place by God to bless you. The words "This whole nation *of you*" refers to the corporate body of Christ.

Brothers and sisters, we need to activate the corporate anointing through our tithing and offering. The devil is doing all that he can to stop that. The word of God clearly tells us,

"Behold, how good and how pleasant it is for brethren to dwell together in unity! It is like the precious oil upon the head, running down on the beard, the beard of Aaron, running down on the edge of his garments. It is like the dew of Hermon, descending upon the mountains of Zion; for there the LORD commanded the blessing – life forevermore."

(Psalm 133:1-3)

It would seem therefore, that blessings can be restricted if we are not in agreement. Subsequently we cannot expect the release of a corporate anointing, when we are in financial disagreement.

> *"For as the body is one and has many members, but all the members of that one body, being many, are one body, so also is Christ."*

(1 Corinthians 12:12)

and

> *"So we, being many, are one body in Christ, and individually members of one another."*

(Romans 12:5)

I personally believe that if the whole body of Christ world-wide, honoured God with His tithe, it would overnight affect the whole world economy, both physically and spiritually. The apparent financial lack over the church of Jesus Christ would be broken totally, completely, once and for all.

Verse 10

> *"'Bring all the tithes into the storehouse, that there may be food in My house, and prove Me now in this,' says the Lord of hosts, 'If I will not open for you the windows of heaven and pour out for you such blessing that there will not be room enough to receive it.'"*

Because the Lord says, *"bring the whole tithe into the Storehouse,"* I take that to mean, *"bring the whole tithe into the storehouse!"* Therefore if we are sending our tithe to another ministry, a charity, or even to friends or family etc, we are not tithing. We are in fact making a ten per cent offering. The act of tithing, is what makes the tithe a tithe. That is, that it goes into the church that we worship at, as Father has asked us to do. If we do not do this, but "send" it elsewhere the tithe then ceases to have "tithe status" and we are in fact making a 10 percent offering. This may have been done in ignorance, but God Himself says, "Bring," (not send) the whole tithe into the storehouse, i.e. the church where you worship. The amount of the tithe is not the important thing that God takes into account, but the obedience in your actions, and that you tithe accurately. Economically speaking, if we all sent the tithe to where we "felt" it should go, the local churches would not function financially, they would just collapse.

> *"For the children of Israel and the children of Levi shall bring the offering of the grain, of the new wine and the oil, to the storerooms where the articles of the sanctuary are, where the priests who minister and the gatekeepers and the singers are; and we will not neglect the house of our God."*
>
> (Nehemiah 10:39)

> *"But when you cross over the Jordan and dwell in the land which the LORD your God is giving you to inherit, and He gives you rest from all your enemies round about, so that you dwell in safety, then there will be the place where the LORD your God chooses to make His name abide. There you shall bring all that I command you: your burnt offerings, your sacrifices, your tithes, the heave offerings of your hand, and all your choice offerings which you vow to the LORD."*
>
> (Deuteronomy 12:11)

As para-church ministries were non-existent at that particular time in history, there was no need to stipulate where the tithe should go other than the storehouse. Nevertheless I firmly believe that we should be building up our local churches financially and corporately, thus activating God's abundance. I believe it to be very much the responsibility of all local churches to support para-church and itinerant ministries. This could be done by churches tithing out, on their own incoming tithes and offerings. This would bring a two-fold blessing, the churches that tithed out, would according to the word of God receive more blessings in return. Also the church or ministry that received a particular church's tithe would be blessed. Can you imagine the dramatic change in church finance that would take place, if every single church and ministry, however large or small, tithed out to another ministry on all its incoming tithes and offerings? If this operation was exercised throughout the Christian church, the "finance" in the Christian world would change overnight. Every church where I have ministered at, and who have then moved into obedience in this area of tithing out from all the tithes and offerings they receive into their ministry have seen added increase. Some even to the payment of the debt on their building.

> *"Then the LORD spoke to Moses, saying, 'Speak thus to the Levites, and say to them: "When you take from the children of Israel the tithes which I have given you from them as your inheritance, then you shall offer up a heave offering of it to the LORD, a tenth of the tithe."'"*
>
> (Numbers 18:25-26)

> *"To bring the firstfruits of our dough, our offerings, the fruit from all kinds of trees, the new wine and oil, to the priests, to the storerooms of the house of our God; and to bring the tithes of our land to the Levites, for the Levites should receive the tithes in all our farming communities. And the priest, the descendant of Aaron, shall be with the Levites when the Levites receive tithes; and the Levites shall bring up a tenth of the tithes to the house of our God, to the rooms of the storehouse."*
>
> (Nehemiah 10:37-38)

"That there may be food in my house" speaks of God's house, the church. The food referred to here, is "sustenance" ("a

means of support": Collins English Dictionary) – money, to sustain the work of God, through the church. The present financial problems that some churches are experiencing, are due solely to the fact that tithing is not being accurately, or regularly, taught from the pulpit. Consequently the body of Christ are just not tithing, nor are most churches tithing out their income to other ministries. This can cause a serious cash flow problem. Malachi 3.10 says, *"Test me in this says the LORD of Hosts."* This is the only time that God actually challenges us to test Him. Try me, test me, prove my word to you, that if you tithe and return to me that which is rightfully mine, *"See if I will not open for you the windows of Heaven, and pour out for you so much blessing that there will not be room enough to receive it."* If God says that He will "open the windows of Heaven" for us then, obviously we **cannot** open them ourselves!

If only 20 percent of Christians worldwide tithe, we must assume that corporately the windows of Heaven are closed 80 percent. This may seem hard to receive, but the fact is this is true. It is time for us the "Church" of Jesus Christ to stand up, shake off passivity, and start being radical with our money.

The key to a supernatural cash flow into our lives, is to be continually obedient in returning God's tithe. Tithing should not be spasmodic, but must be regular, ongoing, and constant, and must be accurately applied to all our income. Tithing will totally transform your lives. It will turn your lives around. Once you commit to faithfully and regularly return to God what is His, the blessings will follow so quickly you will find that you are telling others of the goodness of God that comes from being under an open Heaven.

We need to understand that the blessings are not always necessarily financial. They can be blessings of provision, the new job that you have been seeking, a promotion at work, your business expanding suddenly.

Your personal tithe is completely separate from your business tithe. By submitting your business financially to the Lord, and returning His portion to Him, you will then have placed your self in a position of a two-fold blessing. 1. Your personal income. 2. Your business income. Although you may regard the two incomes as one, there are two centres to be blessed, you and your business! Over the trading period your business will incur costs. Staff, heating, lighting, raw materials, rent, cost of sales, etc. Some business men have seen great growth in turnover and in profit having decided to tithe out on net profit after business overheads have been deducted. After your years trading, and after the net profit has been declared, it is at this point I would suggest that having calculated the tithe you return it.

We have received testimonies that say that healings have been released, that marriages have grown deeper when those concerned have begun to tithe. God rebuking the devourer. Please hear my heart on this, I am not, nor have I ever said that you cannot be healed if you do not tithe, I am simply saying that we have heard testimony from children of God that their healing was released as soon as they began to tithe. For that particular person, the block for them was they were simply not returning to God that which was His. Once you have committed to tithe, that releases the Lord to open the windows of Heaven over you. I have heard of people who once having repented of not tithing, and having made positive confession to tithe, have had their blessings released before they have paid their first tithe. God is willing to move on obedience, that is all it takes – **obedience**.

"When He had been baptized, Jesus came up immediately from the water; and behold, the heavens were opened to Him, and He saw the Spirit of God descending like a dove and alighting upon Him."

(Matthew 3:16)

Look at what happened through Jesus, who was continually under an open heaven. I know by now that you are getting excited, you must be. I am excited for you because I know what is going to happen as you walk in this new-found understanding. You will be blessed. The wonderful thing about being a tither is that we receive an extra blessing from God, available only to tithers. To qualify simply tithe.

Verse 11

"And I will rebuke the devourer for your sakes, so that he will not destroy the fruit of your ground, nor shall the vine fail to bear fruit for you in the field."

Just think about that for a moment. God, The risen Lord, the King over every king, the Lord over every lord, He personally is rebuking the devourer over your lives. The actual act of tithing has great spiritual ramifications. It is a "dynamic." If you do not return to God the 10 percent, when you have received revelation knowledge or teaching about tithing, the loophole that this causes allows the devil the authority to take the 10 percent from you. I do not want that to sound harsh – it's simply a fact! Let's look at the definition of "**rob**":

1. To take another's property unlawfully.
2. To steal something from in any way.
   (Collins English Dictionary)

The word of God says clearly in John 10.10 that Satan is a thief, and that he comes to steal. Therefore if we are knowingly robbing God, our enemy who has been publicly proclaimed by God as a thief has a hold over us in the area of robbery. If we choose to rob from God, Satan can rob and steal from us. When we are obedient to the word of God, we are protected.

"He who dwells in the secret place of the Most High shall abide under the shadow of the Almighty."

(Psalm 91:1)

Absolutely nothing can touch us, when we are in the shadow of God's protection. Our fields are safe – *"so that he will not destroy the fruits of your ground."* Your job, your works, your profits, you will have success in all that you do – *"nor shall the vine fail to bear fruit for you in the field."* In drought, in hard times you will still get your crop.

"There was a famine in the land, besides the first famine that was in the days of Abraham. And Isaac went to Abimelech king of the Philistines, in Gerar. Then the LORD appeared to him and said: 'Do not go down to Egypt; live in the land of which I shall tell you. Dwell in this land, and I will be with you and bless you; for to you and your descendants I give all these lands, and I will perform the oath which I swore to Abraham your father.'"

(Genesis 26:1-3)

"Then Isaac sowed in that land, and reaped in the same year a hundredfold; and the LORD blessed him. The man began to prosper, and continued prospering until he became very prosperous."

(Genesis 26:12-13)

Verse 12

"And all nations will call you blessed, for you will be a delightful land," says the LORD of hosts."

There is no answer to the world's economic problems. Man has tried everything and nothing has worked. Brothers and sisters, we have the power and the authority to change the world economy if we would only obey the word of God. You can change your nation to be a *"delightful land"*. Again consider where God's says,

> *"Return to Me and I will return to you."*
>
> (Malachi 3:7b)

and

> *"For those who honour me, I will honour."*
>
> (1 Samuel 2:30)

Establishing a New Financial Foundation

It may be that you received unclear teaching, possibly even wrong teaching on tithing. It may be that you truly felt that you could not afford to tithe, or even thought that it was okay to tithe only when you could afford to. We now know that we cannot afford not to tithe – whatever the circumstance. If you are married, your spouse should for maximum effect be in agreement with you. If your spouse is at the moment unsaved, then seek the Lord about tithing your own personal finance. Ultimately God is speaking to His children, but this would be an excellent opportunity to prove the goodness of God to an unsaved spouse:

> *"...test Me in this and see if I will not throw open the floodgates of heaven and pour out so much blessing that you will not have room enough for it."*
>
> (Malachi 3:10)

Begin now to establish your new financial foundation, and together let's enter into a new covenant with God about your finance. If you now feel ready to repent of not tithing, and are willing to commit to tithe regularly and accurately on all income that comes into your hands, between now and when the Lord returns, then you are ready to establish a new foundation for your finances. Congratulations.

At this point, or as soon as you are able, read the following prayer. I have already prayed on behalf of each of you who I knew would say this prayer of repentance, and forgiveness. I am standing with you, and rejoice in all that God is about to do for you.

Your Prayer

Dear heavenly Father,

I acknowledge that everything in the earth and the heavens above is Yours. All that I personally have is from You. I thank You for what You have entrusted into my life. I understand now that the tithe is holy, and it is Yours, and belongs to You. I am sorry that I have not returned Your tithe to You.

This day I repent of withholding that which is rightfully Yours. I ask You to please forgive me, and from this day on I commit to tithe on all income that comes into my hands. I now release myself by Your grace from any unpaid tithes from my past.

Thank You Father that Your word says that You have plans to prosper me and not to harm me, and that You will rebuke the devourer. Thank You Father that whom the Son sets free is free indeed.

In Jesus' Name. Amen.

The following is a prayer that I have already prayed in faith for you, after your commitment to tithe.

Dear Father,

I thank you for each man, woman, boy and girl that has prayed the prayer of repentance. I know that you are going to bless them according to your word. You have said that you will rebuke the devourer for their sakes. Father I thank you that in and through the name of The Lord Jesus Christ the windows of heaven are indeed open over their lives. **I now release the blessings and proclaim windows open in Jesus' Name**. Amen.

Blessings are on Their Way

Brothers and sisters, begin to expect your blessings now. Do please remember that as the blessings come in, to give testimony to others, and praise and thank God.

I have at this point left a "faith" space so that you can write down the testimonies of God's blessings in your life as a result of you tithing. Do please pass this book on to a friend, so that they too will have a full understanding of the revelation on tithing and God's personal covenant with us. They will also see from your personal testimonies how God has blessed you, and brought you into new financial freedom.

Please buy another copy of this book, for your own personal reference, and please tell others, as many as you can about tithing. **Get the word out, so that all God's children can walk in abundance.**

And remember, God will bless you...